The Million Dollar Bakery

A story of pursuing your passion & creating the life of your dreams. How I turned my hobby into a million dollar business & how you can too!

REBECCA HAMILTON

Creator and Owner of Chick Boss Cake

The Million Dollar Bakery
Copyright © 2021 by Rebecca Hamilton

All rights reserved. No part of this publication may be reproduced, distributed, or transmitted in any form or by any means, including photocopying, recording, or other electronic or mechanical methods, without the prior written permission of the author, except in the case of brief quotations embodied in critical reviews and certain other non-commercial uses permitted by copyright law.

Tellwell Talent
www.tellwell.ca

ISBN
978-0-2288-5395-4 (Hardcover)
978-0-2288-5394-7 (Paperback)
978-0-2288-5396-1 (eBook)

www.chickbosscake.com

www.rebeccahamiltonco.com

Tune into her podcast called: Scrap The Sweet Talk

Follow her on Instagram: @rebeccaatchickbosscake

Follow her bakery on Instagram: @chickbosscake

Take her online courses, read her blog & check out her services at: www.rebeccahamiltonco.com

Visit her bakery at: www.chickbosscake.com

Dedicated to my Oma and Opa Goettling

My favourite memories were baking in my Oma's tiny trailer kitchen... and with that, Chick Boss Cake was born.

Table of Contents

Chapter 1: How It Started 1

Chapter 2: How It's Going 15

Chapter 3: Forewarning: Business Is a Battlefield 27

Chapter 4: Lesson One: You Are Your Biggest Asset 40

Chapter 5: Lesson Two: Haters vs. Complainers 54

Chapter 6: Lesson Three: Defining Your Values
and Picking the Right People 65

Chapter 7: Lesson Four: Fear Will Paralyze You,
and Waiting Will Kill You 75

Chapter 8: Lesson Five: If You Don't Want to
Quit, You're Doing It Wrong 87

Chapter 9: Lesson Six: It Is ALL of Your Business 103

Chapter 10: Lesson Seven: The Staff Struggle Is Real 115

Chapter 11: Lesson Eight: Confidence Isn't Just
Key, It's Everything 136

Chapter 12: Lesson Nine: Start Creating the
Life of Your Dreams Today 148

Acknowledgments

I have to start off by saying a huge thank you to my husband, Chad, who has always been my number one supporter with anything I've ever decided to do. From my crazy idea of starting a bakery business to writing this book, he always does whatever it takes to support my creative process. I'm forever grateful to be supported by a partner who allows me the freedom to truly be my most authentic and colourful self. Not only does he move mountains to provide me with the time I need to work on all my creative projects, but his enthusiasm and belief in my abilities is remarkable. He has also poured his heart and soul into our bakery business Chick Boss Cake alongside me and is a major contributing factor to its growth and success. As a strong, independent and confident woman, having a partner who complements my strengths and weaknesses is an incredible blessing.

I owe to my strength, tenacity and grit to my parents. Although we've had plenty of ups and downs, I am forever grateful for the gift of life you've given me and for all the tough lessons I learned through the difficulty of growing up in a chaotic household. It took me thirty years to finally understand that you really did do the best you could. There is no doubt in my mind that had I not lived through the chaos and challenges at an early age, I wouldn't be half the woman I am today. It is within that understanding that I found healing, peace and true appreciation for you doing the best that you could. I hope to inspire many people who still hold unresolved anger or resentment toward a difficult childhood or past trauma to heal themselves and stop letting their past dictate the quality of their future. Thank you for doing the best you could; it was everything I ever needed to become the woman I am today, truly.

To my past and present friends, I believe everyone comes into our lives for a greater purpose than that which we understand. If we've ever crossed paths, thank you for being part of my personal journey. I am significantly blessed to currently be surrounded by some of the most generous, beautiful, talented and inspirational women on this planet. Thank you for sharing your lives with me and providing so much joy, encouragement and a safe space to be my authentic self. As an introvert, I thought that *all* people drained my energy and that I didn't need any more "friends." It wasn't until I consciously decided to surround myself with like-minded people who had similar dreams and goals that I realized how much I was missing out on. Whether we end up being part of each other's journey for a lifetime or for a short time, thank you for sharing your journey with me.

And finally, to all the incredible women who have reached out to share their personal stories with me and let me know they've found inspiration in my work, you're the reason I've pursued this path. I had no idea that my words, advice and sharing my personal experiences would resonate with so many of you and inspire you to achieve your dreams just the way I did. Your love, support and loyalty means more to me than you'll ever know, and being able to have a safe space to share my struggles and success with you is more than I could've ever asked for. Thank you for letting me know that I'm making an impact and for helping me to recognize that having an impact is my life's purpose. I'm excited to share this journey with you.

Introduction

As the founder and owner of a million-dollar bakery called Chick Boss Cake, the #1 bakery and dessert spot that all the locals in southwestern Ontario are obsessed with, I know what you're thinking: she *must* be highly educated with some kind of fancy business or baking diploma. Well, I'm not. Sorry to burst your idyllic bubble but if I *did* happen to be armed with the "proper" education or "ideal" upbringing, I wouldn't be writing this book because, well… that never makes for a great story now does it? No one likes to read stories about prestigious, silver-spooned Harvard-educated know-it-alls who achieve success via entitlement and the birth canal of their rich mother. Nah, the best success stories come from someone like me. Allow me to explain…

My childhood and family life were rough. To say the least. My dad had significant anger issues mixed with unrealistic expectations of what a woman *should* be, and my mom put up with it. My loud voice and need to stand up to my parents meant I spent full days and nights at 24/7 coffee shops that I couldn't even afford to purchase a coffee from, sleeping on park benches and staying at sketchy motels where I lived off of cocoa puffs sans milk and those disgusting No Name microwaved chicken slabs that were stuffed with cheese and broccoli. If you're from my hometown of Cambridge, Ontario, The Satellite Motel might mean something to you. That was my home for several weeks until I could no longer afford the $39/night room. Eventually, my friend's mom offered me a place to stay for a few months until I could find a job and an apartment. Bless her heart.

I dropped out of high school at the age of sixteen to move out with my (then) boyfriend. I never set foot in a college or university unless it was to attend a party when I was (very) underage. I got stuck in several unhealthy and abusive relationships and found myself in *plenty* of "what the fuck?" situations along the way. I was angry, depressed, stubborn, riddled with anxiety and basically a runaway freight train trying not to go off the rails.

It was *an absolute fucking nightmare.*

I felt so worthless and low that I seriously contemplated suicide. I had *no* hope. The darkness was real. When I reflect back on that time from where I am now in my warm house and cozy bed, I vividly recall an overnight I spent outside shivering against a constant drizzle that was bone chillingly cold. Cold enough to soak through my clothes and keep me damp and cold throughout the *entire* night. Dying would have put me out of my misery. I blankly stared into the black puddles on the pavement contemplating whether I could continue living at all. Little did I know, that hitting that level of "low" was everything I'd ever need to experience in order to develop the resilience, tenacity and perseverance to create the life I'd always dreamed of.

"It's just a bakery," They said.

"She'll never make it," They said.

"Bakeries don't make any money," They said.

Woah, woah wait a minute. *Who the hell* are "They" and what business do "They" have defining *my* limitations? None. The doubters doubted when I scrapped the idea of a career in policing to open Chick Boss Cake. Maybe they had a right—these are very contrasting career routes, I know. One of the main reasons I wanted to be a police officer was because I had always believed that I needed to have a "real" job. I thought that in order to make a difference or make a decent income, I needed to follow a career path that society deemed to be "reputable" or "significant." Don't get me wrong, I have the utmost respect for public service jobs—police officers, nurses, fire fighters, paramedics—you name it. My issue was that I thought if I *didn't* obtain a career along those lines, I wasn't going to amount to anything. I know there are a lot of people who feel the same way. Peer pressure, family pressure, societal pressure—gosh there's pressure coming at us from every direction—it's no wonder we're terrified to take the leap of faith and shoot for the stars. It's scary enough on its own let alone when you're bombarded with third-party opinions and haters. Fast forward to today, and let me tell you, it was freakin' worth it.

Guess what? It'll be worth it for you too!

I'm going to share my story and struggles with you to explain how I used all that hard shit that felt like the end of the world to catapult myself into the life of my dreams. I am a huge believer that we are not meant to "find ourselves" and instead we need to be *"creating ourselves."* We hold so much power within ourselves that we haven't even discovered or tapped into yet, and I'm here to help you access the unlimited potential you've unknowingly had all along.

Let's get something out of the way first. If you're looking for a "sit back, manifest and that's it" kinda book, this is *not* for you! I don't believe in merely "thinking things into fruition" in hopes they "magically appear" one day. It's lazy. I'm taking a wild guess that since you picked up this book, you're not where you want to be.

Am I right? I feel like I'm right.

That approach will *never* truly get you to where you *actually* want to be. Don't get me wrong, I believe in manifestation, visualizing and the whole "universe provides" approach—BUT—the thing that all those other books are missing is the cold hard reality check.

You *must* put in the work!

The work involves a whole lot of self development, reflection, healing and growing. I'm here to keep it real and share my personal story of how I built a million-dollar bakery business from nothing but pure grit and tenacity when no one believed in me. If I can create *this* much success with a little bakery in small-town Ontario, with zero education or formal training then you can do it within *any* industry. I know it!

This book is for everyone who's been through the worst and is still here against all odds.

It's for the woman who lost her voice but knows the world *needs* to hear what she has to say.

It's for the wife who pursued a career that society made her feel was the *only* respectable option.

It's for the girl who settled down too soon instead of chasing her wild and crazy dreams that everyone laughed at.

It's for the entrepreneur-at-heart who shows up every day to their soul-crushing 9-5 job feeling unfulfilled instead of pursuing their passion and igniting the fire within.

This is *my* story of how I created the life of my dreams, and there ain't no sugar-coating it (bakery puns are essential in this book, FYI). I'm going to take you through the exact steps I took to grow my business to one million in sales so you can learn how to do it too. I'll be sharing my personal stories, struggles and everything I've learned along the way so you can learn from them and apply my best practices to your own business. You do not need to take the longer, more difficult road to success when everything you need to know is between these pages. In order for you to truly change your life and business, I've included lessons for you to complete throughout the book. If you want to change your life and business, you need to *actually* do the work.

By reading this book, you will not only gain a concrete understanding of the best business practices, how to deal with haters, what to do about complaining customers, how to manage staff and how to push through your fears, but you're going to gain the confidence and awareness on how to intentionally start creating the life of your dreams. Once you know my secrets, you're not going to be able to go back to your mediocre life; you're going to become the artist of your own life. You're about to embark on the greatest journey of all time, so get ready to take action and watch your masterpiece *come alive*—yep just like the song from *The Greatest Showman*.

Nothing fulfills my heart and soul more than helping other entrepreneurs and fellow business owners discover their true potential and achieve massive success beyond their wildest dreams. My latest business venture, Rebecca Hamilton Co. (www.rebeccahamiltonco.com), is devoted directly to this. You'll be able to connect with me there where I share plenty more business and life tips and lead you in creating the business and life of your dreams!

It's time to open your heart and mind to endless possibilities and get ready to unlock your true potential. The world needs who you were made to be, so stop withholding your greatness and step into your power! Just a forewarning before we continue: as the title of my podcast *Scrap the Sweet Talk* suggests, I'm here to keep it real with you. This book is completely unfiltered, uncensored, raw and full of life-changing lessons that I *know* are going to inspire you.

Shit's about to get real.

Are you ready?

Chapter One

How It Started

I enjoyed baking and decorating as a hobby, but I'd never seriously considered it as a career choice. Ever. The earliest memories I have of baking are alongside my Oma in her tiny trailer kitchen. She had this famous family cheesecake recipe that we always made together. Rule 101 of baking with Oma: I always got to lick the spoon. As children, many of us have those people in our lives that we're obsessed with (in the best, most innocent way possible), and she was it for me. My favourite person.

I had Oma in my mind when I climbed into my Ford Mustang that my boyfriend, Chad (who has since been promoted to husband), picked me up in for my lunch break from the shelter for abused women where I worked. We rolled up to the nearest Tim Hortons and sat in the parking lot staring at all the interesting people coming and going. Watching strangers is always so intriguing to me. I always wonder what their lives are like or what their dreams are—I'm a curious person. When he asked me how work was, I unleashed an unusual and choppy response filled with long, awkward pauses.

"Work is fine. I don't think I want to pursue a policing career anymore. I hate running. I hate the stupid beep test. My co-worker told me I'm good at baking and said I should start a bakery. I'd always loved baking with Oma growing up..."

(Long, awkward pause)

"It sounds so stupid," I continued. "There's no way I'd make any money running a bakery. I'm probably not going to do it. I should stick to my goal of being a cop. It's more of a 'real' job."

(Longer, more awkward pause)

"But maybe we should just *try* doing a home-based bakery business on the side," I said. "I don't know. What do you think? Tell me if it's stupid."

"I think you should do whatever makes you happy," he said after a brief pause to digest my word-vomit.

Obviously, the right answer. It was the first time he had heard anything about this "bakery" idea, so the fact that his response wasn't "What the hell are you thinking?" was definitely refreshing. He'd always been the most encouraging and supportive person I'd ever known—a stark contrast from the egocentric dudes I'd dated in the past.

So, there it was—the initial idea of starting a bakery came from my favourite memories of baking with Oma paired with a random conversation with a co-worker only to evolve into a semi-serious discussion in a Tim Hortons' parking lot. Makes me wonder what other things are started in Tim Hortons' parking lots... actually, I *don't* want to know.

I never really knew what to say when someone asked me what I wanted to do for the rest of my life. It's such a soul-sucking, permanent question. It's as if a career is a "life sentence." I *never* knew what I wanted to do, and I flip-flopped on my answers often. Seven-year-old Rebecca wanted to be the Dickie Dee man—yep, the ice cream dude on a bike; talk about goals. It was a reflection of my deep love for sweets that made it such a favourable career path then. If you asked fourteen-year-old Rebecca, she would have said "actress" or "Spice Girl." Or both. How original. Every fourteen-year-old's dream back in 2006 was the same. I also went through a hairdresser phase before I decided to take a step back and figure something out. So policing was the *final* answer.

Until it wasn't.

The thing is, I had this perception that a career was something you *had to do* for the rest of your life. I researched different careers, what they paid and what working it for the rest of my life might look like. It freaked me the hell out. I don't care who you are. No one wants to make the "wrong" decision and regret feeling stuck in a career they can't stand. Based on my personality and what I thought I would be good at, I decided to pursue a career in policing. I found out it didn't require any further schooling—a deal breaker for me because I hated everything about school—so it seemed very achievable. I had forgotten that my God-given gift is creativity, which is not high on the list for a career in law enforcement.

My attempt at becoming a police officer was cute. I ate healthy, worked out every day (sometimes twice), studied and took several "practise" exams. I even went to the police college where they run free trials of their fitness tests to see where I was at. Let's just say athleticism was not my gift. The harder I trained, the more I hated it. It was making me miserable.

That day in the parking lot at Tim's, I decided to take a break from policing and take a flyer on my stupid bakery idea. Since I was only working part-time at the women's shelter, I had plenty of free time to try it out and see where it led me. Worst case scenario, family and friends would enjoy the taste-testing process and appreciate some extra baked goods along the way.

The first step was coming up with a name. Ah, yes. The question I get most often: where did you come up with the name Chick Boss Cake? Oddly enough, Chad came up with it. We went back and forth for weeks. How hard is it to name a freakin' bakery? Hard. I didn't want a "fluffy" name like Rebecca's Sweets, Treats and Confectioneries—no offence. It's just not my style. I also didn't want something cheesy like Whisk Me Away, Baking Memories or Batter than Yesterday. I totally made those up and profusely apologize if they're legit names (they probably are somewhere). There's nothing wrong with them, but they're not my style. I needed a little bit of edge, and I wanted it to *mean* something.

I cultivated my first real love for cake decorating watching the TLC show *Cake Boss*. I learned everything from watching that show. I was mesmerized by what Buddy was able to do with cakes and it lit my soul on fire.

"You're basically the female version of him," Chad said between mouthfuls of my latest experimental cupcake recipe. "How about Chick Boss Cake?"

I was flattered but definitely nowhere near as talented as him. Also, doesn't "chick" offend people these days? I certainly didn't want to offend anyone, but the more I thought about it, the more it grew on me. *What the hell?* I thought. *Let's go with Chick Boss Cake.* It was conceived as a small home-based business anyway—I had no plans of taking it seriously. It wasn't like it would be on billboards or store signs or anything like that…

Three locations and a massive billboard later, Chick Boss Cake is engrained in the minds of our loyal customers for life.

Sorry/not sorry.

It's no secret that the name isn't my favourite, but I also don't know what else it would be now that it's everything it is. It suits the personality, brand and me—fun with a little bit of edge!

OK, how about some research into whether I was even allowed to have a home-based bakery business? Good next step. I hadn't a freaking clue. I made a zillion phone calls to find out what I needed to do to follow the rules. Remember, I wanted to be a police officer so I'm an extremely ethical person and have a strong desire to always "do the right thing." After a ridiculous amount of prying straight, factual answers from the city and health unit, I understood that different counties have different regulations as far as home-based businesses. We lived in an apartment in London, Ontario, which did not allow it.

So—obviously—I moved to the closest area where there were no by-laws (at the time) preventing me from operating a home-based business. Hello "Progressive by Nature" Elgin County. Chad and I found the perfect cute little country house where the owners were renting out their basement. As a side hustle—more like a hobby, in fact—I seriously did not think this business would expand as rapidly as it did. That's right, I literally packed up and moved my life for a side hustle hobby because I'm a die hard rule follower. If you know what the Enneagram test is, I'm a 1 Wing 8. So, that about sums it up. Here we were, living in this basement apartment twenty minutes outside of the London city limits just to ensure my *hobby* was not breaking any rules.

Word started to get around about my business, and friends of friends began ordering from me. Before I knew it, it was earning me more money than my part-time job. Eventually, Chad and I got married and bought our first home in St. Thomas, Ontario, where I continued my little hobby bakery business from home. Chad was working full-time in stock trading at TD, and I was still picking up part-time shifts at the shelter.

The challenging thing that nobody tells you when operating a home-based business is that you don't have anywhere to meet customers. Even as an introvert, I knew I'd eventually need a space to meet with customers and grow the business. I don't know about you, but I watch way too many murder mysteries on *Dateline* to just let random strangers frequent my home. We always delivered products to our customers, and if they asked where we were located we dodged the question. No one really cared *that* much but, when it came down to it, I really just wanted a shop to call my own where I could have customers visit for wedding cake tastings and give everyone an epic experience. My heart and intuition was telling me it was time to take this thing seriously…

One major problem was that my health was shit. Physically, I actually *appeared* to have been in the best shape of my life due to all my police training, but mentally and emotionally I was wrecked. I literally could not wake up in the morning earlier than 11:00 a.m., and I required a mid-day nap. It was so awful, and I had no explanation. I was far from lazy, but I was plagued with daily brain fog and just could not function. It was debilitating. I wouldn't even make plans with friends or family in advance for fear that I would have to cancel due to my energy levels. It seems crazy, but the saddest part is that I chalked it up as part of my "personality"—as if zombie is a personality trait—for many years. There was absolutely no way in hell I would be able to run a business where I had to physically open the doors at a specific time in the morning. Absolutely not.

This insane lack of energy had affected my entire life. When I was younger, I couldn't get up for school in the mornings, and even on the days that I did, I just couldn't function properly. I was exhausted from simply waking up. How does that even happen?

My mom would struggle to get me out of bed for school in the morning, and my dad would drive me to school. We would stop at Tim Hortons on the way to get me a triple triple coffee (isn't that the preference of every teenager?) and a chocolate chip muffin. Breakfast of freaking champions right there. After he drove off from dropping me at school, I turned around immediately and took the bus home and went back to sleep. I couldn't make this up if I tried. It was so ridiculous. Of course, I felt guilty for pretending I was going to school, and I knew it wasn't exactly going to get me straight A's, but I literally just *needed* to sleep. You're probably wondering why my parents didn't notice or do anything to help. Well, they had plenty of their own significant issues to deal with that overshadowed what initially appeared to be a sleepy teenager who hated going to school.

If it wasn't for Chad, I would have continued to think feeling like shit was completely normal. His energy and motivation made me curious. Actually, it kind of drove me nuts. Probably because I was jealous that he had an abundance of excess energy while I had *none*. Do you know how draining it can be to live with someone with that level of energy? You need energy in order to be around people with energy. I figured it was just his personality, but he couldn't understand how someone who slept so much *still* had so little energy. It didn't make much sense, so he encouraged me to see my doctor.

After describing my symptoms, my doctor handed me a prescription for anti-depressants. I mean, he wasn't wrong. I was also *very* depressed. How can you not be when you have no energy or motivation to function? The lack of energy kept me in this vicious cycle of hopelessness. It truly was hard to get out of bed every day, and the struggle was real when it took all my energy to simply get dressed and shower. I didn't know if I was depressed because I had no energy or if I had no energy because I was depressed. I took the meds for a week and they made me feel substantially worse, so I ditched them. I know you're supposed to take them for longer than a week before you notice any benefits, but I just couldn't. I was desperate to figure out what was happening, so I did what every concerned adolescent does: I Googled it. I read other people's symptoms and stories and found a common thread: get rid of gluten.

I had legit never heard of the word "gluten" before my amateur anecdotal Google search. The deeper I dove down the Google rabbit hole, the more I started to believe I might have an *actual* allergy to gluten. I was eating a lot of it—some days that's all I ate. Most people make a few small changes since it's not their primary source of fuel, but I would have to change my entire diet. I reflected on my upbringing and was shocked at how much gluten I ate growing up. "You are what you eat," as they say.

Well, shit!

As much as bread, pasta and cereal were my go-to foods, I was desperate. I'd do anything, including cutting them from my diet. So, I went cold turkey and ended my lifelong love affair with gluten. Forever. The results were *seriously* life changing and almost instantaneous. It took about two weeks of not eating *any* gluten whatsoever before I experienced an insane amount of energy and a new zest for life. If this happened for me, how many other people had been duped by the gluten lie? How many other people were depressed and thought it was their personality? Don't get me wrong, depression is real, but the food choices we make have a huge impact on our energy and overall well-being. I have not touched gluten to this day. Except for the schnitzel incident in Germany—oh my God I almost died—but that's a conversation for another time over a glass of wine.

I felt unstoppable. Well, almost unstoppable. When I initially went gluten free, I didn't know early on if it was a permanent solution or a temporary fix—only time would tell—so I proceeded with caution. The extra energy gave me the boost I needed to finally quit my part-time job at the shelter and open my first actual bakery store location. I was skeptical and didn't trust my own body to function properly because the endless amounts of energy were brand new and kind of scary, so I decided to keep my store hours short just in case I couldn't handle it. I'd open at 12:00 p.m. and close at 6:00 p.m. That's right, my initial store hours were p.m. to p.m. There was *no way* I could commit to anything greater because of my health. How sad is it that I believed my well-being and energy would be taken away? So freaking sad. All I wanted was to feel good, be happy and have energy to do the things I loved.

My first store opened July 25, 2015. Yep, it was the first Chick Boss Cake sign hanging in all its bright pink glory on the main downtown strip of Talbot Street in St. Thomas, Ontario. The first time the public got a true taste of our now famous Cotton Candy Lemonade (where the straw is buried beneath an exorbitant mound of cotton candy), Chai Cheesecake Hot Chocolate (where an actual slice of cheesecake sits on top of the drink), our creative and colourful doughnut collections and of course our whimsical cakes and cupcakes. The reception was insane and resulted in line-ups out the door and down the street.

We ended our first week with a fabulous Grand Opening celebration at the shop! Many loyal customers who had previously ordered from my home-based business showed up, along with friends and a few family members. My aunt and uncle were there and, while they were excited for me, they mentioned that my Oma and Opa were not doing well. They had been in a long-term care home for a little while, but they'd also always been doing OK. It was devastating news, but I wasn't sure of the severity of the situation. At the time, I wasn't on speaking terms with my parents, so my aunt and uncle were my only source of information regarding my Oma and Opa.

"Should I call them?" I asked.

"You need to go see them," said my aunt.

My brother and I went so neither of us had to go alone. Opa was unresponsive when we arrived. I'd never seen him like that before, and the prognosis didn't look good for him. He'd always been totally "with it," witty, extremely strong and exceptionally stubborn. The nurse told us outside his room that they were moving him into palliative care. I didn't know what that meant, so it crushed the nurse's soul when she had to explain that they would keep him comfortable and pain free as he died.

Devastated doesn't begin to describe my feelings. I had dreaded this day my *entire* life. From the first moment I learned what death was as a child, I feared the day my Oma and Opa would die. Of course, I knew it would happen, but I also knew I'd *never* be ready. I constantly worried as a child that any visit I had with them could've been my last—as if I was trying to mentally prepare myself for that day. Deep down I knew no amount of preparation would prepare my heart for such devastation. Any time my parents brought me to visit them, I would always insist on sleeping over and spending as much time with them as I was allowed to. My Oma and Opa always brought me so much safety and comfort in a childhood that didn't always feel that way. Even as I write this, I can't help but uncontrollably sob my way through the sentences. As tough as it is for me to write these words, it's important that you know how my worst nightmare was unfolding just as I'd taken a huge leap of faith in opening my first store. I sat in the long-term care room in silence the rest of the day; it was comforting just breathing the same air as them.

While my Oma wasn't the one going into palliative care, she wasn't fully "present" either. She slept a lot. My parents showed up. I hadn't talked to them since before my wedding four years prior (that they didn't attend), so that was awful and awkward. For the record, my parents aren't *awful* people; they just had their own issues going on when I was growing up, and they often got in the way of our relationship. More on that later.

My Opa died a week later, and I was lucky enough to be in the room as he took his final breath. My lovely therapist encouraged me to go see him as much as I could that final week even though it tore me apart to see him like that. I don't know what gave me that kind of courage. This was the first time I'd ever experienced a family death, and what an experience it was bearing witness to the exact moment one of the most important people in my life passed away. The strongest, most "if you want something done right, you better do it yourself" person I'd ever known.

My Oma passed away only eleven days later. Thankfully, Chad was able to take a couple of weeks off from TD to run the storefront because there was no way I would have been able to help people in the state I was in. The only time I've ever closed my store outside its regular hours was for their funeral. I was an emotional wreck for *months*, but I didn't take any days off; there's no bereavement or sick days when you're self-employed. Plus, I had *just* opened and couldn't afford time off. I showed up to work every day and worked in the back. I had cakes to do and people were counting on *me* to do them. I'll never forget one of the cakes I made during this tough time. It was for a ninety-second birthday, which was close to my Opa's age. I remember thinking how special it was that his family had ordered him a beautiful cake, and I had to ensure it was perfect.

That was my experience opening my first Chick Boss Cake location. Needless to say, overcoming the worst thing I could imagine made me so strong and powerful. Deep down, I feel it was my Oma and Opa's way of contributing to my resiliency one more time before leaving this earth. It was as if they timed it perfectly to push me to a make or break point (and I know that they had a mysterious and spiritual way of knowing that it was going to *make* me).

Chad joined my business full-time about a year and a half after opening our first St. Thomas location. He had always helped out with the business whenever he could—before and after work or on his days off. He was at the top of his game at TD, and let me tell you, they made it extremely difficult to part ways with their generous benefits and stable income, but we had always planned on him joining me to run Chick Boss Cake together long-term. We thought the logical time for him to quit the bank and join me in the kitchen would be once our sales matched what he was making at TD. The problem was that I needed help. Like, yesterday! It was getting too busy for me to run the business *and* make the products *and* help customers all by myself. Not even my new-found gluten-free energy was enough to keep up. We tried to hire a lady to help out at the shop in the meantime, and she was wonderful most days but had her own personal struggles that made her inconsistent… and consistency is key in business. She was truly a kind soul and our first *real* employee. I'll always have a special place in my heart for her, but I needed Chad's help. So, he turned in his button up shirts and business attire for an apron and ball cap, rolled up his sleeves and immersed himself in the world of baking.

Within six months of Chad leaving his job at TD, he was making the same income at Chick Boss Cake that he was at TD. He was an expert sales guy (in the most kind and genuine way possible) and an extrovert—the complete opposite of me. We complemented each other perfectly. I'm not going to lie: the idea of working with my husband freaked me the hell out. What if we broke up or got divorced? What if we *hated* working together? I'd heard nothing but horror stories about getting into business with your spouse. Even friends would casually say they could never work with their partner. I remember thinking to myself, *Well, why the hell did you marry them if you don't enjoy being around them?* Don't get me wrong, there were plenty of people I had dated previous to Chad that I could never ever ever work with… but Chad seemed different. The truth is, I didn't really know if it was the stupidest idea I'd ever had or the best idea I'd ever had, but I was willing to take the risk to find out.

REBECCA HAMILTON

Chapter Two
How It's Going

    Obviously, the title of this book is a pretty good indication of how it's going. But it explains nothing about how I actually *got* to this point. It doesn't speak to the sleepless nights, the tears of frustration or endless number of times I almost called it quits.

    That's *why* this book is so important to me. The universe called upon me to share my experience and everything I've learned with you. I feel a duty and obligation to walk you through my failures and teach you that success is not solely for people who graduated from Harvard or experienced an ideal upbringing. It's also for the people like *me* and *you* who have no idea what the hell we're doing. It's for those who dropped out of high school and/or had a rough childhood but continued to bust their asses to fulfill their dreams despite it.

    I feel like every small business' first monumental goal is to get to one million in sales. It certainly was for me, but it seemed way too far-fetched even for a goal getter like me. Compared to a several billion-dollar company, a million may sound like peanuts, but that massive company initially had a goal of a million bucks before it got there. A million is just one of those numbers that speaks for itself and proves that people love your products and are interested in your business. You don't get to a million in sales if no one cares about your product or your business. You also don't get there without resilience, tough skin, gratitude, confidence, tenacity, grit and a stellar team.

Our London, Ontario, location opened about four years after we opened our first store in St. Thomas. Four years is *way* too long to remain in one stagnant spot with your business—especially if you have big goals and dreams like I did. Of course, we had our reasons why we stayed in the same spot for years—all derived from fear.

Fear of failing.

Fear of scaling too quickly.

Fear of not hiring the right staff.

Fear of not knowing what the hell we were doing.

Legit fears. The problem is, when we base decisions around fear, we'll never get to where we want to go. In fact, fear will hold us back 150% of the time. We can't rationalize our fears and convince ourselves that they "make sense." Fears are almost always made up. Anything and everything worth having is always always *always* on the other side of fear. If you're not fearful then your goals are not big enough.

So, if you learn just one thing from this book it is to take action right now. Don't wait. Even failure is a better option than being paralyzed by fear. At least failure offers lessons and the opportunity to try again, whereas taking shelter in your comfort zone does absolutely nothing but provide you with a false sense of temporary relief. We spent four fucking years trying to figure out the "safest" and most "practical" way to grow our business. Oh boy. It makes me cringe to reflect on that archaic thought process. It was totally out of line with my goals.

During our four years in St. Thomas, staffing was interesting to say the least. I don't know why no one ever talks about this, but staff are the most difficult *and* most important part of building a sustainable business. We finally took the leap and opened London because we struggled to find qualified people in St. Thomas; it was just too small of a town and none of the applicants who were applying for a job had any experience working in a commercial kitchen. If you've ever worked in a commercial kitchen, you know that it's quite a shock to the system. It's hot, busy and requires attentive focus and precision when following recipes. Not to mention how physically demanding it is being on your feet all day. And don't get me started on the raw and brittle skin that envelops your hands from washing them (and dishes) twenty-five billion times a day. I eventually came to the realization that since there weren't many places around town for people to gain experience or the skills required for a bakery job, it was up to us to figure something out. So, we decided to invest in training them from scratch ourselves. Yes, you can train the fundamental skills of baking and cake decorating, but training is also expensive and does not guarantee that they're going to stick around or enjoy the job. I found that most applicants had this false fantasy of what working at a bakery would look like: spending all day meticulously baking one perfect cake while time stood still; perfectly placing sprinkles one by one where they felt most inspired to place them. Shit, we'd be long out of business if that's what working in a bakery was really like. One measly cake a day would *not* pay the bills.

There was a huge disconnect between the expectations of the applicants and the reality of the fast-paced, production line of cakes that needed to be done in a timely manner in order to produce any kind of profit and be able to issue them a paycheque. We made an honest effort to hire the people who were applying without any experience working in a commercial kitchen since we didn't really have a choice. Plus, during their interview, they'd often proclaim their endless love for baking with grandma in the kitchen as a kid—something I could relate to. *Great!* I thought. *Shouldn't be too hard to train them.* Except they didn't come equipped with the same grit and work ethic I'd developed. They'd constantly proclaim that working in a bakery was harder than they thought. Well, no shit. The struggle was *absolutely* real when we started trying to build our team. No one cares about your business the way you do.

The frustration of building a "winning team" in a small town of 38,000 was substantial. Don't get me wrong, there are many pros to opening a business in a small town, but finding qualified people with a very specific skill set is *not* one of them. It's no fault of their own, but there's just nowhere for them to gain the experience and exceptional work ethic they need to succeed in such an environment. We'd repeatedly hire one or two people, and they would either quit or get fired. Then we would be back to just Chad and I, which, albeit easier to manage, was impossible to scale. We always found ourselves struggling to justify paying an employee when we could just do it ourselves. Did you know that the majority of small business owners run their business solo because they have the exact same issues and mentality of "I'll just do it myself"? It's true. You could just do it yourself, but you'll never scale or *grow* it by yourself. You need people. We needed people. More than that, we needed great people who were just as excited, driven and ambitious as we were… or at least close to it.

Not *everyone* we hired in the beginning was awful, but the good ones were very hard to come by. It wasn't always their fault either. Remember when I said we didn't know what we were doing?

We had no idea how to manage staff. I was under the impression that people who were applying for a job, get this—*actually* wanted one and that in order to keep it they had to show up and—wait for it—*actually work*. We had the illusion that managing staff meant that the biggest challenges we'd face would be trying to work around sick days and scheduling time-off requests. Illusion is right! It required *so much* more than that. We eventually realized it was helping them through the days when they just don't *feel* like working, talking them through their bad moods, listening to their family issues, sympathizing when they break up with their boyfriends, supporting them through their mental-health struggles and communicating it all in a way that makes sense to them on their level. I hadn't even considered having to do this on top of the millions of other job duties like providing exceptional customer service, handling complaints, making all the products, answering the phones, writing the emails, marketing the business, staying active on social media, completing deliveries, scheduling and all the rest of it. I was under the impression that we were hiring people to help the workload and not add to it. Managing is an art form—a balancing act at its finest. You need to find the perfect balance of "shit needs to get done" and genuine care for your employees' well-being. It starts with finding the *right* people who align with your values, but we didn't know this in the beginning. And it showed.

We're firm believers that if something isn't working, try something new. So at one point, we decided to do something drastically different and hired a crew of five people at once and train them in specific roles. We thought maybe if they only had one simple job to focus on without a lot of multitasking they might be more successful and at least find the job easier. This was a very logically smart decision except we still were hiring the wrong kind of people. We seemed to attract people who did not share the same values of kindness, gratitude, integrity and passion that we did.

Our values were not clearly defined, so we didn't know what to look for in an employee. I'm pretty sure the universe ensured that we hired an endless number of the wrong people in the beginning to demonstrate the qualities we weren't looking for so we'd know the right ones when they came around. Kind of like dating all the wrong people until you understand what you *don't* want.

That's when the universe nudged me. My gut told me we needed to open a store in London; it was only thirty minutes from our St. Thomas location, but the population was 500,000. It's hard to describe, but I just felt it, and I knew it was going to be the right decision. Logically, there was a much larger pool of prospective employees to choose from there, and there were places that people could work within our industry to gain experience and skill, not to mention there was even a baking and pastry arts program at Fanshawe College. I knew that there *had* to be better qualified people there that would take this job seriously and share our values. I had never been the "risk-taker" in our relationship until this point, and it was obvious that it freaked Chad out. He'd never seen me so excited or dead serious about a decision before, but a woman's intuition is *never* wrong, so we went for it.

The hilarious part about opening our next store in London was that we had two employees at the time and the rent of our London location was *six times* more expensive than St. Thomas. We were going to need a much bigger team to produce six times the amount of product and pay our rent. I basically had no staff, no money and no idea what I was doing.

But I had full faith in my plan and was ready to be the risk-taker.

Fast forward to now, and it was definitely the right decision. Chick Boss Cake London has been open for a couple of years, and we've built a stellar team of truly talented individuals who value their job and thrive in our upbeat, positive and kind culture. They're my kind of people. These are the types of people you need to have as part of your winning team. Like-minded, goal-oriented and genuinely kind people who share similar values. Naturally, we still face challenges with staff from time to time, but overall we've been able to find people who share our vision, are motivated to grow their career with us and are excited to share in the success. We spent about a year and a half in London ironing out many policies and procedures and ensuring all systems were as efficient as we could make them before opening our third location in Woodstock, Ontario.

We opened Woodstock right smack dab in the middle of COVID-19. It could have been a smart decision or not so smart—I wasn't sure. At the beginning of 2020, before COVID-19 was even a big deal here, we had planned on opening our third location *somewhere* and at *some point* that year. We were going back and forth between a few different locations, and Woodstock wasn't one of them. It seemed too small because we wanted to set up shop in a bigger city with loads of potential room to grow. We put up a poll on our Facebook page asking where the next Chick Boss Cake location should be, and we were surprised that Woodstock was top of the list. When COVID-19 finally started wreaking havoc in our area, naturally we put the idea of opening a third store on pause because we didn't know what impact it would have on our business—or if we'd even *have* a business when it was all said and done. It wasn't long before the government took drastic measures by closing down major cities, airports, businesses, schools and events. COVID-19 reality was starting to set in. Every day from the beginning of the global lockdown, I was consumed by *so* much chaos and confusion. The lack of control and clarity was *terrifying*. I was starting to get anxious…

When the government ordered everything to close except for "essential services," I didn't know what to do. Were we considered "take-out food" (an essential service)? I don't know. Not *really*. But we could be if we needed to be, right? I didn't know what the right thing to do was, and the Enneagram 1 wing 8 in me was nervous about breaking rules. Naturally, I did what I always did when it came to big, important decisions—go with my gut and make sure we followed the rules to the T. My gut told me to stay open unless someone literally knocked on my door telling us we absolutely must close. The last thing I wanted to have happen was to close up shop too early only to be *forced* to close weeks later. There's no way I was going to willingly close my business without being forced to. So we modestly stocked up on gloves, masks, sanitizer and toilet paper and did the only thing we confidently knew how to do: *hustle*!

One of the hardest parts of navigating this global pandemic was leading a team of employees through it. If building and managing a team during *normal* circumstances was challenging, how on earth would I learn to do it during a global pandemic? Here's how: the same way I've learned everything else in life and business. Face it head-on and navigate it together with kindness, honesty, humility and trust in my gut.

We gave our team the option to either work through it alongside us or stay home with no hard feelings and come back when they felt comfortable. There was no right or wrong decision because no one really knew the answers. A few staff stayed home and the rest decided to work until we *potentially* got closed down and were *forced* to stay home. Thankfully, we were never forced to fully close; we stayed open for take-out and delivery the entire time.

Not knowing what the future looked like, Chad and I decided to go full freaking force through COVID-19 like a Mac truck (or more realistically a cake delivery truck). While other businesses were scaling back on everything including advertising, staffing and hours, we ramped ours up. We thought that we might have to close down any day, and we weren't going down without a fight. I was stuck in that sick-to-your-stomach fight-or-flight mode for *weeks* while praying every night for the health and well-being of my family, friends and staff.

Turns out that kind of stress is awful for your body and immune system—not exactly what I was going for during a global pandemic. It made me even more nervous that I might be making myself sick by carrying that much stress in my body; talk about a vicious cycle. But the stress eventually turned to excitement because we were SO busy. Busy beyond my wildest dreams. During those first couple of months, Chad and I worked every waking second—*literally*. If we slept for seven hours, we worked the remaining seventeen, seven days a week, for a solid *four months*.

Our staff were *not* far off from that either, and many of them worked longer and harder than ever before. We were so fortunate to have these amazing humans along for the ride on our team. Everyone was doing *everything*. They switched their roles and took on duties that weren't even a thing before. Deliveries and packaging orders—jobs that didn't exist before March 2020— became full time jobs. If we could have hired during that time it would have been ideal, but it was too risky to bring anyone else in during such chaos and uncertainty.

We tried to make it fun for everyone along the way. With the increase in health and safety rules, we relaxed our company rules a bit. We let them use their cell phones, got everyone food several times, got them grocery gift cards and even scrapped the regular Disney music for some Pitbull and 90s rap... the storefront was closed after all and *nothing* is more motivating than Pitbull and 90s rap. Oh, and during a time when people weren't allowed to see people, it was such a blessing to come to work and be around my incredible team. They're the most fun, and they lightened up the long, dark days of COVID-19.

We were so grateful to deliver delicious treats and happiness to everyone being forced to quarantine at home. Our customers were so gracious and patient with us as we fumbled through trying our absolute hardest to just make it to the next day. I'm a perfectionist. Always have been, always will be. It's in my blood. *Nothing* about this was perfect. We had to miss calls, emails and live chats for several days on end. Initially, we got flooded with emails from brides postponing their wedding cakes, parents calling off their kids' parties and many customers who had questions about their orders that we didn't have answers to. We had to figure it all out on the spot as things came up, and it was imperative that we prioritized how we handled the workload in a way that did not jeopardize our business. Staying open and healthy was number one, sales number two.

Among all this chaos, it occurred to us that a substantial number of our deliveries were going to Woodstock, Ontario. Hmmm… I thought back to the poll. Shoot, those people were right. We had a huge following of loyal customers in this area. But who takes risks during a global pandemic? I mean, it just seemed plain stupid. I remember thinking, *I don't think this COVID-19 thing is going to be over any time soon. Who knows how long it will last? It could be years.* The last thing I was prepared to do was put my goals on pause for another couple of years— or longer—because who *actually* knows? Once I came to that realization, I decided we may as well go for it. We had that *"now or never"* mentality, and if it failed at least we'd learn something from it. *No one* teaches you how to navigate your life or business through a global pandemic. So, we did it. We opened our third location in Woodstock, Ontario. And guess what? It's been the best performing store out of all three stores despite the shutdown. Often, the most difficult decisions end up being the best decisions!

We've essentially doubled our sales year over year. You can only have substantial growth if you're willing to take substantial *risks*. Having the intuition to make great choices is a gift, but there are plenty of valuable skills, lessons and tangible pieces of advice I've learned along the way that I *know* will help you along your journey. They're not Harvard accredited, but they're real and unconventional ways that offer a fresh perspective through the lens of real-life struggles and overcoming tough shit. I hope they'll help you grow as a person, take bigger risks, become a better leader, turn your hobby into a business, grow your small business to one million in sales and create the life of your dreams.

Your time is now!

REBECCA HAMILTON

Chapter Three

Forewarning: Business Is a Battlefield

Business is a freaking battlefield. It's not the cute "Boss Babe" T-shirts or "Chick Boss" brand or "Girl Boss" coffee mug, although I certainly adore all the cute little glamourized swag. It is *not* cute pinstripe pants, perfectly ironed button-up shirts, blue lens glasses, top knot buns or sipping margaritas on Wednesdays because you get to "make your own schedule." It's none of those things, and it certainly is anything *but* glamorous.

Allow me to paint you a *real* picture of what running a business looks like. It's working 24/7 making literally no money for the first *few* years, running on no sleep, trying to fill twenty-five different roles, keeping your cool with customers in between meltdowns, breakdowns and boiling points. It's facing criticism from haters, turning down nights out with friends, fearing failure every day, doubting yourself, wondering why you started and contemplating how much more you can take all while your family and friends live within the comforts of something called society where they sleepwalk through their simple daily lives, work eight measly hours a day (usually 9-5), make a decent income with two weeks paid vacation and enjoy weekends off indulging in something called hobbies and interests.

Running a business literally feels like you've been chewed up, spit out and booed off stage. Or wait, that's an Eminem song… still, it's a legit description of the life of an entrepreneur. Scared yet? Didn't think so. You're strong and also just as nuts as I am to think any of that shit sounds like a good idea. What part sounded appealing to you? Zero sleep? What about no money and working 24/7? Do you want to deep six your social life? I am not trying to discourage you from starting or growing your business (although if you do find yourself discouraged already then do yourself a favour and quit while you're ahead). If any of that made you second guess your business or the possibility of pursuing one, then you weren't built for running a business. See, entrepreneurs are crazy enough to read that and still want to pursue it anyways. If you don't want to quit 1000 times over again, then you're definitely doing it wrong. I'll be the first to admit, it all sounds insane. Because *it is*.

Here are the four most important things you need to armour yourself with so you can enter the battlefield confidently.

Be a Goal Digger

First and foremost, you need to set your goals and align them with the right expectations. The first thing I always ask people when helping them build or grow their business is what their goals are. I need to have the end game in mind before offering *any* kind of advice or feedback. I can tell right away if their goals are misaligned if they say something along the lines of: "I want to make millions of dollars, have complete freedom and also have a great family/life balance and spend tons of time with my kids." I hope you can see the misalignment and unrealistic expectations. If not, I'm here to help you with that.

In my experience, business people fall into one of two categories: ones who want to take it to the top and ones who don't. I'm not saying the latter is bad or wrong, but you need to know which category you fall into. If you want to take your business to the top and grow and achieve great success with ultimate freedom and financial security, you're totally aligned with me. If you want to run a small business where you just make a decent living while upholding your family work/life balance then that's OK as long as you understand that you cannot have both. The amount of work involved in creating a super successful business with a million in sales is ultimately endless. The needs of your business will not cut you any slack or care that you have to miss another one of Bobby's hockey practices. Be realistic about your goals, expectations and the amount of work you're willing to invest to get you the results you envision. If you have a stronger desire for a family/life balance, don't set your goal to make millions of dollars and take the business to the top. Nobody that's made that kind of money and achieved that level of success avoided sacrificing family and leisure time to get there. It's true that you could potentially make a decent living by running your own small business and making family life a priority, but it's still going to be significantly more work and longer hours than if you simply had a 9-5 job at the bank. So, just be prepared.

If you're feeling depression, unhappiness, unfulfillment or anything along those lines it's likely due to misaligned goals (unless, of course, you have a diagnosis or medical condition, which I trust you're seeking advice from a professional on). See, when we say we want something and then fail to do what it takes to make it happen, we feel like a failure and we feel really bad about ourselves. This happens in all areas of life where you might have a goal but don't yet have the desire to work toward achieving it.

Let me give you an example. You want to lose weight but you keep eating like crap. You're telling yourself you *want* to lose weight and yet not taking necessary steps to make it actually happen, leaving you feeling even fatter and more like a failure than before you set that goal. You're better off being more honest with yourself and saying that you're fine with being overweight and in fact you *love* your curves. This way, you're not battling against yourself with your goals vs. the actions you're actually willing to take. Whenever we are at war with ourselves we feel unhappy, uneasy, unfulfilled and depressed.

Have you set goals where you weren't actually doing anything to achieve them? Now is the time to re-evaluate. Simply by being honest with yourself and saying you're not ready to put in the work it will take will be a relief. The way you talk to yourself matters and has a substantial impact on your overall well-being and happiness. Never underestimate the power of positive self-talk and learning to truly love yourself.

So, go ahead and tell me what you want, what you really, really want... is my Spice Girl throwback revealing my age? Ah well... they *did* say it best! What do you really want? Get super clear on the specifics. I want details of the life you envision for yourself, what kind of house you want to live in, what kind of car you want to drive, where you want to vacation. What does your life look like once you've achieved your goals? Paint a very clear picture in order to get to where you want to be and so you know when you get there. You can truly have anything you've ever dreamed of if you do everything it takes to get it. The problem is that people just want all these things without doing any of the work. Not exactly how the world works, my friend. Nothing is more irritating than people saying how lucky I am to have the life that I do. Of course I'm grateful for my life and everything I've created, but I worked my ass off and cried in corners on the sticky un-mopped floor praying for the strength to get me through the next day (more on this story later). I pulled all-nighters and stood on my feet for hours on end. It had nothing to do with *luck* and everything to do with what I was willing to sacrifice to achieve my goals and make my dreams a reality.

News Flash: Money Actually Does Buy Happiness

Feel weird and uncomfortable being honest about your love and desire for money and financial freedom? I hate when people say "Money doesn't buy you happiness." The fact is, money buys us time. Time to do things that *make* us happy and fill our souls. Thus, money can buy us happiness. We're either trading money or we're trading time, so the more money we have, the more time we'll be able to buy. Why is money such an uncomfortable topic? It's a common, fundamental part of our society, yet it makes some people sweat having a simple conversation about it. Some folks feel awful admitting that they want, like or love money. If you all didn't love money and want more of it (or at least love what money provides) why the heck do you go to work every day? I mean, seriously. It's so weird to me that some people get flustered when this topic comes up. Anyone I've ever talked to about money always has to follow the conversation with: "But money isn't everything and it doesn't buy happiness." Sorry, what? Why do we even feel the need to follow up with a statement like that as if the other person is judging us for talking about a common currency that keeps our society going, feeds our families, provides a cozy roof over our heads, allows us to travel and explore the world and—oh yeah—buys freaking pets! I don't know about you, but the most obvious form of money buying happiness is my two dogs that cost me *money* to purchase them. Have kids? What about the diapers, formula, top-of-the-line hospitals to give birth in, Pinterest-worthy nursery? Did any of those things come for free? No. Not even the top-of-the-line hospital that we pay taxes for.

"Money can't buy happiness" was misconstrued down the lines of communication. Remember that game called Telephone where you're sitting in a circle and one person starts by whispering a message and the next person tries to say the same message to the next person? The same thing happened with this message. Someone started by saying something like, "Money isn't the only thing that provides happiness. In order to live a truly fulfilled life a human also needs love and connection in conjunction with money. All of those things combined create happiness and fulfillment." I'm pretty sure that's actually how the conversation went, at least that's what I tell myself because that's what I believe. Money isn't a *replacement* for love and connection, it's an equal. It's just as important. If society wasn't set up to run solely on hard currency, perhaps my opinion would differ. Money just happens to be the currency that humans exchange for fundamentals like shelter and food. Thus, it is essential to our existence.

I constantly hear people say, "Money changed him" or "Yeah, my great aunt is loaded and she's such a terrible person." Listen, money is powerful, but it's important to note that it is a *tool* and nothing more. It doesn't have the power to make someone a bad person or a good person. It's impartial because it's simply a tool. It's how people *use* the tool that makes them a good or bad person. Having a little or a lot of money has absolutely zero to do with anything other than the fact that you either have a little or a lot of money. Sara Blakely, an outrageously wealthy businesswoman, entrepreneur and philanthropist, says that money just makes you more of the same person you already are. In other words, if you're a kind, generous, grateful person, you'll be just that except with more money. Same goes if you're a greedy, mean, angry, spiteful person; you'll still be that same person just with more money.

Another reason you may have a bad relationship with money is because you judge and are jealous of people who have it. If you find yourself uttering comments about people on Instagram that you don't even know like: "Oh yeah, she thinks she's such a big deal because of the car she drives," or "He must be such a jerk, look at him flaunting all this money,"—news flash—you don't even *know* them. You're judging them because you don't have those things and you want them. You're jealous and letting your insecurities convince you that money is evil. Pay attention to every time you start judging someone else for anything—their appearance, life, partner, car, house, whatever—and you'll notice you're just trying to make yourself feel better and less insecure about the areas your life is lacking. I believe in the law of attraction and manifestation, so if that stuff freaks you out, sorry/not sorry because it actually works (provided you put in the work). If you're constantly feeling insecure and telling yourself that money doesn't buy happiness to try to make yourself feel better, you're just pushing it further away. Keep saying how much you don't want it or need it and you'll *never* have it. Which, I guess, is what you "say" you want, but I think you're just saying that to try to fit in and because you think it's the polite thing to say.

What would happen if you stopped pushing money away and started manifesting it instead? I'm going to assume you think you're a good person otherwise you wouldn't be reading this book because, well, I doubt evil masterminds are interested in reading my life and business books. So, if you're a good person and you start manifesting money, what would happen? That's right, you'll be a good person with *more* money! Does more money mean your family would be taken care of better and experience less stress and worry? Does it mean your kids could go to a better school? Does it mean you can volunteer your time more often with causes that matter to you? Does it mean you'd be able to afford larger donations to the charities you care about? I'm pretty sure it does. See, money allows you the opportunity to focus on the love and connection part of life. That's why they're all equally important. If you don't have money or pretend to not care that you don't have money, you'll have less of it resulting in having to work harder and longer with less time and energy to enjoy your life and all the meaningful things in it. Next time someone says money doesn't buy happiness, send them a copy of my book and remind them of this philosophy. It might just change their perspective, and it could even change their life.

One of my favourite people to learn how to manifest money and have a guilt-free relationship with it is author and business mogul Grant Cardone. He's very straight forward and aggressive in his approach. While his personality might be too much for some people, there's a lot we can learn from him. I personally love his 10X conferences—Chad and I have watched them all. They're great! He's taught me to fearlessly chase my goals by putting in ten times the effort. Once I learned his 10X approach to business, I was able to take bigger risks and push through my comfort zone in massive ways.

For example, I'm an introvert by nature, and I used it as an excuse for not networking, creating connections and doing things that made me uncomfortable. When I applied his 10X approach, I decided I was going to break free from my introverted comfort zone (which, in hindsight, was extremely fucking boring). I took a public speaking course, started a podcast, went to networking events, made several new connections and started producing videos that shared my tips and advice publicly. That's like, a lot. Especially from the stark contrast of doing none of those things—ever. If I was going to step outside my comfort zone prior to learning the 10X approach, I would have only tried doing one of those things. Instead, I decided to go all in, commit to my goals and put in ten times the effort I normally would. By doing all those things, I'm a completely different person now. Yes, I'm still an introvert by nature, but I've truly expanded outside my comfort zone and have a new-found love and appreciation for connections and sharing my thoughts via videos or my podcast called *Scrap the Sweet Talk*.

Another person I love is writer, speaker and success coach Jen Sincero. She wrote a great book called *You Are a Badass at Making Money* where she talks about the struggles she's overcome in her relationship with money. I loved this book a lot, and she's a very entertaining writer. She'll make you laugh. I highly recommend it. She was the first woman I'd ever seen openly talk about how she loves money and how to change our preconceived negative association with money. Once I was able to overcome the ingrained scarcity mindset I grew up with and change my relationship with money, the money showed up. Just like she said it would. The mantra she offers in her book is: "Money flows to me easily and freely."

Remember, money is a tool, and tools are used to build things. Manifest the money and stop feeling guilty about it. Stop talking negatively about it and pushing it further away. Use this tool to build your empire so you can help advocate for world issues that you're passionate about. The world needs more kind, grateful, generous, caring people who have the money to change it!

The Secret to Success: Get Your Shit Together

The more you work on self-development and becoming the strongest, best version of yourself, the better you'll be able to battle through adversities. You'll read a little about my childhood in the coming chapters and how those tough times earned me the strength I need to push through all the business challenges. I highly recommend healing from any past pain and trauma and turning it into resilience, grit and strength instead of fear, weakness and sorrow. Stop reliving past pain because you haven't made healing a priority. Maybe you actually had a great childhood and didn't experience any kind of trauma or particularly difficult situations. Well, you're not off the hook. In fact, you might just need the most help when it comes to overcoming obstacles in business. If you want to build and grow a successful business, embarking on your own personal self-development journey will be a gigantic asset. How can you expect your business to grow if *you're* not growing? Learning the best practices for dealing with stress, creating healthy routines, developing emotional intelligence and learning how to handle other people's emotional fluctuations are all things we need to work on. The best advice I can give you is to be obsessed with becoming the best version of yourself. Read all the books, listen to all the podcasts, attend all the conferences and take all the online courses. Do all the things! Invest in yourself. You can only take your business as far as you've been able to take yourself.

Find Your Obsession and Get Support

Before you start your business or take your existing business to the next level, make sure you're *so* passionate about it. Just like a life partner, you'll need some deep-rooted love to pull you through the hard times. You know, the kind of love that pulls you through the relationship hurdles such as the dirty socks under the bed, loud chewing of bananas right next to you and leaving the toilet seat up… or are those just my own pet peeves? I feel like I'm not alone on those. My point is, if you're not obsessed and truly in love with your business then when shit gets difficult, you'll quit instead of pushing through. You need the deep-rooted love for what you do to keep you from throwing in the towel. Make sure it fills your soul and provides you with fulfillment.

Speaking of life partners, make sure that if you have one that they are supportive of you and your dreams. If they're not, I'm sorry to tell you that one of them is not going to work. It's up to you to decide if it's the business or the partner that needs to go. A business is difficult enough without having to deal with constant fighting and lack of support at home. Your partner can have their own job and do their own thing while you do yours, but they need to unreservedly bring the support, love and encouragement. You don't *have* to work together, although it really works great for Chad and I since we have opposite personalities and skills. If you're able to work together and you both have opposite strengths, then do it. You'll be able to get twice as much done and grow twice as quickly.

My tips for working together and not killing each other? Simple. Always treat each other with kindness and respect. It really is that simple. Also, clearly define your job descriptions and responsibilities and stick with them. Try not to interfere with what those responsibilities are either; you don't want to be constantly stepping on each other's toes. Working together can be the biggest blessing if you treat it as such.

If you don't have a spouse or they don't want to join your business venture, you'll eventually want to find a business partner. I can't imagine doing this on my own and making my own decisions without bouncing ideas off a like-minded individual. It would be so lonely. If you plan to grow past a million in sales then you'll need someone who cares about the business and has the same goals in mind to help you with it. Plus, achieving success is so much more fun alongside someone you truly care about. You can't make a toast to yourself!

There are a few key things to look for when auditioning business partners. First and foremost, make sure they're reliable. Don't partner with your flaky college friend who constantly changes their plans. There's nothing worse than trying to run a business alongside someone who may or may not show up when you need them.

Next, you'll want to target someone with a contrasting skill. Don't partner with someone exactly like you who has the exact same skill set. You don't need two of the same people, you need someone who is better and more skilled in areas you're weaker in. By sharing different skill sets you can each focus on your strengths. A business depends on the quiet, introverted, creative product developer (hint: me) just as much as it needs the extroverted, sales and people management person (hint: Chad).

While complementary personalities are key, you'll want to ensure your core values align with your partner. This is essential in life and in business. If you want kids and your partner doesn't, that's generally a deal breaker in most relationships. If your business partner wants to spend evenings and weekends with family regardless of the fluctuating needs of the business, and you're all-in and willing to work at all hours to ensure its success, it's only a matter of time before you realize your values don't align. Misaligned values always lead to friction and resentment, which is not a solid foundation for a successful business.

Finally, make sure the person you partner with is just as obsessed with your business as you are. Like, if you're running a stellar butcher shop, it's probably not a great idea to partner with your vegan friend, Jess, you know what I mean? Passion and obsession will make or break your business. Both you and your business partner need to be obsessed. No one ever became successful by pursuing something that was of mediocre interest to them. Make sure your business lights your soul on fucking fire!

I told you I was going to keep it real with you throughout this book, and I have. You need to learn how to actually *do* business, as in the action of doing business not the conceptualized textbook crap they teach you in school. The art of doing business is not complicated—in fact, it's 20% skills and 80% psychology. By constantly developing ourselves and making our well-being a priority, we have the energy, stamina and mental clarity we need to maintain optimal performance.

That brings me to the next chapter, the one where my life changed forever and where yours can too.

The Million Dollar Bakery

Chapter Four

Lesson One: You Are Your Biggest Asset

Nothing will work unless *we* do. If we're not taking the absolute best care of ourselves physically, mentally and emotionally, nothing else matters. We'll never have the energy to operate a business if we don't make healthy living a priority. Even if your energy level seems fine, introducing healthier habits will make a substantial difference in your energy level. Running a business is freaking exhausting and way more work than the typical 9-5, so we'll never succeed without intentionally creating and sticking to healthy habits.

Eat Like Shit, Feel Like Shit

There is *no way* I would have reached the level of success I have without treating my diet as a non-negotiable. No way in hell! My health issues were pretty drastic prior to going gluten free. I couldn't wake up in the mornings, and when I rolled out of bed in the late afternoon I *still* had no energy to do even the smallest of tasks. I used to suffer from debilitating brain fog to the point where I couldn't focus or put together proper sentences. It was awful and such an uncomfortable time.

Going gluten free changed my life—literally. I'm not suggesting that *everyone* should go gluten free, but I am suggesting you re-evaluate the food you're putting in your body. Don't try to convince yourself that you're not eating that badly. If you're not intentionally planning your meals and following a consistent diet filled with food that actually gives you energy and makes you feel good, then you're not eating that well either.

I'm not a doctor—unless there's a cake emergency and it's falling apart, in which case I can perform a mean double icing, bypass sprinkle surgery. In all seriousness, always consult a doctor before making any drastic changes to your diet. Having said that, you don't need a medical degree to understand that humans need to fuel their bodies with food that generates optimal performance. What you eat directly impacts your energy, mental state and emotional well-being. Don't believe me? Try it.

Start by figuring out what diet works best for you. One diet does not fit all, as food affects people differently. However, the basics are the same:

- limit sugar (and you know that's serious when it's coming from a bakery owner)

- increase your vegetable intake

- drink at least half your body weight in ounces of water every day

- absolutely no fast food

The rest is up to you to figure out. These fundamentals can be added to any diet variation. If carbs actually make you feel good and give you energy, then eat carbs. Just because your BFF follows a keto diet does not mean you have to. Pay attention to foods that cause bloating, gas and digestive issues, and straight-up avoid them. Your body uses several ways to tell you that what you're eating is not right, so if you pay attention, you will figure it out.

We're meant to feel energized, satiated and alive, not sluggish, foggy, constantly tired, bloated or uncomfortable. Any time we feel less than energized and fuelled, something is wrong. We are obligated to figure out the diet that works for us and maintain it at all costs. This is our life we're talking about here, and as far as I know, we only get one.

I'm so passionate about healthy eating because I've seen first hand what the changes have created in my life. Changing my diet was crucial to my ability to grow and scale my business. I'm a completely different person to the one I was pre-gluten free. I'm not even talking in terms of weight loss either, although if you do consistently stick to a diet that makes you feel great, you'll naturally shed some extra pounds. I'm currently a size 12/14, and size isn't even the most important part; the most important part is energy level and feeling good on a consistent basis. Think about it, if you're 70 lb. overweight, imagine picking up seventy pounds of weights at the gym and walking around with it. You'll eventually feel tired and won't be able to keep carrying it. It will naturally drain your energy quicker than if you didn't carry the extra weight. I did this myself. I lost 50 lb. and tried carrying a fifty-pound weight around the gym with me one time—it's heavy. It really made me think about the fact that carrying a substantial amount of excess weight on my body was a lot of extra work and energy.

It's especially important to eat food you *know* makes you feel good when you have something important coming up. I can't tell you how many times I've had a conference, concert or trip planned and "celebrated" by going out to eat. Obviously, *no one* celebrates with a freaking salad, so you go for the quesadilla with a side of sweet potato fries. No! Bad idea. If you're going to have an unhealthy cheat meal, plan for it on a date that *doesn't* matter, like a random weekend you're chilling at home. Do not—I repeat, do not—eat these types of meals when you need to feel your best. It might seem boring or lame to eat healthy during times of celebration or on vacation but trust me, you'll enjoy yourself so much more and won't need to spend the next day (or two) in recovery mode taking shots of Pepto Bismol.

I'm saying this because I genuinely care about you, and I've been on the opposite side. Chad and I have travelled the world together and been to some of the most exotic and remote places on the planet. Looking back, that time was *so precious* and so valuable but—no joke—I probably spent half the time sick in the hotel room. Who else can relate to feeling worse on vacation at times because we stuff anything and everything into our mouths? Maybe this is why they say you need a vacation after your vacation. This is precious time completely wasted because I didn't understand the connection between eating healthy food and feeling good. I could have easily prevented it had I known better. Once I discovered this connection, I decided that feeling good was a higher priority than eating something that tasted good. Naturally, I have a substantial sweet tooth, so I treat myself once and a while. But I mostly replace all my treats with healthier versions.

I owe my success to my diet. It's allowed me to come alive and start truly living a life full of energy. I feel better than I ever have. If you take only one thing from reading this book it's to take your diet and health seriously from this point on and make it your personal mission to feel energized and fabulous *every single day!*

Mental and Emotional Well-Being

A healthy diet isn't the only thing that's essential for a successful entrepreneur. Taking care of our emotional and mental well-being is also extremely important. When these three elements are not aligned, we have a very difficult time getting to and remaining at the top of our game.

A key factor is sleep. Maintain a set bedtime and stick with it. Not having enough sleep kills energy, and our brains will not function at top capacity. Take sleep seriously starting now.

Becoming successful takes a substantial amount of effort. In order to have success, we must make physical, emotional and mental well-being the top of our priority list. Nothing else can take their place, and we're in full control of those areas. Any reasons we come up with that might get in the way are called excuses.

Excuses are bullshit. Stop making them.

Excuses are lies we tell ourselves so we don't feel guilty for not doing the things we know we *should* be doing. Write that statement down and reflect on it daily. Eating a healthy diet *also* aids in our emotional and mental well-being, but there are additional things we can do to gain optimal wellness as I will mention below.

Cut Out Negative People

Cut, limit or drastically reduce the time you spend with negative people. They'll bring you down 100% of the time. Cut as many negative people out of your life as you possibly can and don't feel bad about doing it because I can guarantee that most negative people do not want to be around you either. Positive people annoy the hell out of negative people, and vice versa. If you can't fully cut these people out of your life because you have an emotional attachment to them, I get it, but I suggest you substantially decrease the time you spend around them.

In addition to decreasing your time around them, also adjust your expectations of them. Do not seek advice or feedback from these people on your new wellness journey or anything you're doing to enhance your life. Do not share your dreams and goals with them unless you're prepared to be judged or crushed. Adjust your expectations of these negative people if you plan on keeping them in your life because they're never going to see things in a positive light. They'll have a problem for every solution. So, keep the conversation to a minimum—short and sweet.

Meditate

Adopt a meditation practice. I know, meditation can sound like this weird hippy dippy thing, but it's not. There's a reason why the most successful people in the world meditate—it works! It helps to clear my mind and puts me in a calm state of being. Challenges will always come our way, there's no avoiding them, but when we face them with a calm, meditative mind, we can resolve the challenges quicker and with less effort than if we hadn't meditated.

In addition, if you're trying to start or grow a business you'll need to take the time to calm your mind in order to see things clearly and be able to make strong, thoughtful decisions. The best decisions and most creative ideas come from a calm and cared for mind.

Scrap Other People's Opinions

Other people's opinions don't matter when it comes to living your best life. Generally, the people closest to you will be the most uncomfortable with your self-development journey. This can make it difficult because, naturally, you'll be excited that everything you're doing is for the betterment of your life, so how can anyone perceive it as anything other than wonderful? Well… the thing is, when we make positive changes in our lives they can make the people closest to us feel insecure about the lack of action in their own lives. Some people are uncomfortable with change since it can alter aspects of the relationship they previously enjoyed and loved.

For example, if your friend Brenda looks forward to your weekly wine and pizza night and all of a sudden you tell her you're on a health journey that doesn't align with wine and pizza night, naturally she'll feel disappointed. Wine and pizza night was the highlight of Brenda's week. Maybe she'd be open to doing it monthly instead of weekly. Perhaps a weekly activity that doesn't involve food might be a good option. Nonetheless, as silly as it might sound, she may need some time to mourn the "old you" and accept and adjust to the "new you."

Your job is to stick to your healthy new lifestyle regardless of the opinions or reactions of anyone else. Not even the people closest to you should have the power to derail you from living your best life. You're in charge and the power belongs to you and only you.

Be Stronger Than Your Excuses

Excuses are the worst. They turn us into weak, flimsy people. The problem is, it's so *easy* to make excuses, give in to excuses and be derailed by excuses, which is crazy because excuses aren't even real. We make them up based on what society wants us to believe to be true. Excuses are what we tell ourselves in an attempt to justify not doing what we know we should be doing.

Here's some common excuses:

I'm too tired.

I don't have enough time.

My schedule doesn't allow for it.

I have kids.

I don't feel like it.

I could go on. Do any of these sound familiar? They do to me! I'm guilty of using some of these excuses, too—we all are—but I've learned to pay attention to them and call myself out on this type of bullshit. We're so quick to judge other people, but why waste time doing that when we have so much work to do ourselves? Once we start paying attention to the excuses, we can identify them more frequently and change them to a more honest statement.

For example, if I was to use the excuse that I don't have enough time, I would stop, be honest and say, "I do have enough time. I have the same amount of time in a day as everyone else, and other people manage to make time for this. My lack of time is a result of poor planning on my part, and I need to prioritize and plan my day better." That statement is the truth, and the excuse of not having enough time is just that—an excuse. You'll notice the more you commit to yourself and your goals, the less you'll need to monitor for excuses and the stronger you'll become. The results you get are a direct reflection of the choices you make. If you make strong, powerful choices, you'll get strong, powerful results.

Invest In Yourself

You are your biggest asset and best investment. Yes, that's right—YOU! To put it bluntly, if you're not *here* then nothing else in your life matters. Think about that for a second. I hate nothing more than hearing how women feel guilty or selfish for taking time, money or energy and investing in themselves.

Please, for the love of God, stop believing this.

Where did this belief even come from? Probably from back in the day when women weren't allowed to work or vote… Well, times have changed, darling, and so must your old-school beliefs! When you become a better version of yourself, *everyone* benefits. Your kids have a *better* mom, your husband has a *better* wife, your parents have a *better* daughter, your best friend has a *better* best friend, your business partner has a *better* business partner.

Get it? Got it? Good.

How do you become a better version of yourself? I'm glad you asked. You spend your time, money and energy on things like business conferences, self-development books, wellness retreats and anything that will help you develop and grow.

A Morning Routine Is a Must

Develop a sacrosanct morning routine. In case you've never heard the word "sacrosanct" before, the definition is: "regarded as too important or valuable to be interfered with." Intentionally creating a morning routine that inspires you to be the best version of yourself is essential to your success. Successful people *all* have morning routines because it helps them start their day with purpose, passion and intention. There's no question that successful people have an enormous amount of responsibility (naturally, I mean you don't just become successful by doing nothing). So, you could imagine how they might feel if they just rolled out of bed after hitting snooze twenty-five times, skipped breakfast, fuelled up solely on caffeine and rushed out the door. I'm willing to bet they would be moody, tired and lacking the necessary amount of energy to power through their day.

A set-you-up-for-success morning routine should consist of the following key points:

- Write down your goals for the day
- Set your intentions

- Develop a gratitude practice

- Drink a decent amount of water

I'll add bonus points if you implement a healthy breakfast, a meditation practice or anything else wellness based into your routine. Go online and research what other super successful people do during their morning routines and try adding some of their practices into yours to see if you enjoy them. There's so many amazing and successful people out there and, while they all might do their morning routine a bit differently, they all have the one thing in common: they *have* a morning routine!

OK, it's time to get started. Grab a notebook or some loose-leaf and your favourite writing implement and answer these questions. I suggest keeping all of the answers together with the book and accessible for when you want to review. Maybe a folder or a binder would be appropriate.

Lesson One Exercises:

1. Cut out negative people. Make a list of the negative people in your life. The people who constantly complain, make you feel bad or bring you down.

    Now write down which ones you can cut out completely. You don't owe them an explanation, just stop making plans with them.

    Then take note of the ones whom you do not want to cut and write down five ways you'll limit the amount of time you spend with them. It could be as simple as meeting them for a quick lunch break coffee instead of going to their house for dinner and spending the entire evening together.

2. Meditate. Download a meditation app like Head Space (my personal fav) and start with a daily five-minute meditation. Consistency is always more important than intensity, so don't try to do an hour-long meditation one day and then forget about it the rest of the month. You'll achieve better results from shorter, more consistent meditating rather than longer sporadic meditations scattered throughout your month. Start small and work your way to longer ones.

3. Scrap other people's opinions. Make a list of the people closest to you and write down things you've done together in the past that may not align with your new goals.

    Now write down alternative activities you could both do together so you'll have suggestions to offer them next time they invite you over to wine and pizza night.

    True friends will want to support your growth and development journey even though it may cause a slight inconvenience to them. Anyone who doesn't support you could be moved into the negative people category.

4. Be stronger than your excuses. This should be easy. Create a list of common excuses you make or—better yet—ask yourself why you're not doing the things you know you need to be doing to live your best life. These "reasons" are *actually* excuses in disguise.

   Once you have your list of go-to excuses, write down three foolproof actions you'll take for every excuse you wrote down.

   Most importantly: abide by those actions at all costs. Be stronger than your excuses!

5. Invest in yourself. There are many ways other than financial that you can invest in yourself. You've already started by picking up this book! In fact, reading any self-development or wellness-based books are helpful. The next step could be exploring the free education and self development advice on the internet, specifically the YouTube goldmine.

   If you can afford to, I highly recommend investing in self-development or business conferences. I've attended many (virtually and in person), and they're worth the money every single time. A few of my favourite conferences were "Rise" by Rachel Hollis, "10X Growth Conference" by Grant Cardone, and "Unleash the Power Within" by Tony Robbins.

6. Morning routine. First, you need to figure out if you have time in the morning or if you need to make time in the morning. If you don't usually have a lot of free time to work with and you constantly have a million things to do before rushing out the door, start by setting your alarm an hour earlier than you normally would. If this means you go to bed an hour earlier than you normally would, then so be it.

Second, write down what you envision your ideal morning routine to look like.

Try it out for several days and make adjustments as needed.

Above all else, make sure you stick to it. Running around like a crazy person does not count as a routine. I've tried and can confirm that it doesn't work.

The Million Dollar Bakery

Chapter Five

Lesson Two: Haters vs. Complainers

There's haters here. There's haters there. No matter where you look, there's haters everywhere! Oops… wrong book; This isn't Dr. Seuss, but I totally just made myself laugh and thought it was the most accurate and appropriate way to start this chapter because haters are literally everywhere. They'll *always* be everywhere. So, if you can't change the fact that there's haters *everywhere* it means you can only change two things:

1. Yourself.

2. Your approach to how you handle situations.

Remember, you're never in control of what other people think, say or do. You only have control over what *you* think, say or do.

So, you want to be successful, huh? I'm guessing you're only looking on the bright side of success and haven't given much thought to the dark side. That's OK, I totally get it. We're positive people who focus on the positive side of things. The problem is, there's always pros and cons to every situation, and I feel like people don't take a second to acknowledge the cons that come along with creating substantial amounts of success. It's true that success amplifies a lot of things—your income, customer base, positive reviews, network and brand—but along with amplifying the good, it also amplifies the bad. This includes your haters, negative reviews and everything else that all the negative people in the world choose to focus their energy on. This applies to business and to life.

Yes, of course people will love you, what you stand for and what you have to offer the world. But they will also hate you, everything you stand for and what you have to offer the world. I know, it's insane because you're a kind and genuine person who cares about the greater good, babies, dogs and world peace; who on earth can hate on that? The answer: Someone, somewhere who hates happy people, the bright and cheery colour yellow, watching people succeed and has deep rooted issues (and takes them out on you). You need to *know* and be prepared that no matter how hard you work, how talented you are, how much you contribute to society, there's always "those" people who don't give a shit and don't like you no matter what.

Don't spend your valuable time and precious energy trying to convince them otherwise because they clearly don't share your values. I know this is a tough one, but the more awesome and successful you become, the more intensely you'll be loved *and* hated. Are you prepared to settle for a small and limited amount of success in order to have fewer haters, or would you rather have a million-dollar company with a higher volume of haters? I'll take the latter, thank you very much.

One of my favourite quotes of all time is by Brené Brown, a professor, lecturer, author and podcast host. She says, "If you're not in the arena also getting your ass kicked, I'm not interested in your feedback." She means don't listen to the haters who aren't chasing their dreams and working hard to achieve them.

Here are my tips on dealing with haters and complainers.

Learn the Difference between Haters and Complainers

There is a substantial difference between haters and unhappy customers. You can't blanket everyone who doesn't love your products as a "hater." Haters hold *no value* whatsoever and are mean people projecting their own insecurities onto innocent bystanders. Unhappy customers, on the other hand, provide helpful insight into areas of your business that could be worth improving upon. In fact, unhappy customers, or "complainers," often hold the *most* valuable feedback that has the potential to take your business to the next level of greatness. The majority of haters have never even tried your product or service but just heard from a friend of a friend that you were awful so it *must* be true. This speaks directly to their intelligence level. Unhappy customers are just that: customers. They've either *bought* your product or *tried* your service.

I totally get it. Haters and unhappy customers both suck the same amount, but if you're able to separate yourself from the initial hurt you feel when someone doesn't like your product or service, you'll be able to take valuable feedback and implement it to improve your business. Obviously, positive feedback is wonderful (and totally preferred—I get it, trust me), but it'll never help you to grow or improve, and there is *always* room for that.

Look at a company like Apple, for example. They have some of the smartest people in the world working for them, and you'd think they'd be able to develop the next best thing on their own. But they can't because if the customer doesn't like it then the customer isn't going to buy it. Companies that are *that* big are constantly digging for customer feedback and even paying for it.

They have departments that send out customer satisfaction surveys and then analyze the data in order to improve and roll out the next best thing. If you want to be successful and a big deal, learn from the big guys.

How to Deal with Complainers

If you have customers going out of their way to send you negative feedback, value it and send them a heartfelt thank you for the insight they provided (whether you agree with it or not). Remember, *you* still get to decide if the feedback is worth making a change or not, but without *any* feedback you wouldn't even have the opportunity. Here's the process I use.

1. Be quiet and listen first. What are they saying?

2. Analyze it to understand where they're coming from and determine whether there is any merit to their feedback.

3. Look for common trends in the feedback that customers provide. Is there a main issue that people *keep* complaining about? If so, address the root cause and implement a solution to avoid that complaint.

We make changes based on frequent and common complaints all the time. It's up to us to pay attention and make the connection between valuable insight and someone's randomly odd opinion. In the very beginning when I started baking from home, I was using this vanilla cake recipe I'd found in a pretty Pinterest-worthy bakery book from Chapters. You'd think a book as pretty as that would surely have a stellar vanilla cake recipe, right? Wrong. We consistently received feedback that the cake was dry and flavourless—not exactly what we were going for. As an avid chocolate lover, I'd just assumed that vanilla cake was supposed to taste like nothing. Evidently, it's supposed to taste like vanilla, so we had to do better. We used the customer feedback to develop a stellar vanilla cake recipe that is as vanilla-y as it gets. Super moist and delicious. Almost good enough to convert chocoholics like me—*almost.*

If they're complaining about something that is *your* mistake, it needs to be fixed or compensated appropriately. If your staff accidentally mixed up the orders and gave Karen the drunk Barbie bachelorette-themed cake for her kid's fourth birthday instead of the Sesame Street one she ordered... Well, I'm sure you can conclude how well that went. Funny enough the lady who ordered the bachelorette cake but accidentally got the Sesame Street cake was actually more pissed off. I guess a drunk Elmo cake doesn't have the same effect. Whatever the issue is, if it's your business' fault, you have two options:

1. You go out of your way to fix it at no cost or inconvenience to the customer.

2. You provide a full refund or credit toward their next purchase.

Owning your mistakes and providing sensible solutions in favour of the customer will build trust and loyalty.

How to Deal with Haters

As previously mentioned, haters are useless. So, I only have one tip on dealing with them:

1. Don't waste your time or energy.

Do not engage with them. You'll never win because they have endless time and energy to waste on useless shit and you *don't*. You've got a business to run and an empire to build! Also, delete and block them from *everything*. If they hate on you once, they'll do it again. You owe it to nobody to give haters the platform and opportunity to hate on your pages or social feeds. Delete, block, repeat!

Customers Have the Choice to Work with You, and Vice Versa

Did you know that doing business with someone is a two-way street? You would've never guessed it based on the traditional Walmart "the customer is always right" policy. (By the way, I've got no hard feelings against Walmart, even if they've created a few entitled Franken-customers along the way.) Customers have the choice to work with you, and, believe it or not, you have the same choice when it comes to working with them. This shocks a lot of people, but it's true.

It's even more true when you're offering a service in the form of art. Not *everyone* will be the right fit for your style or products, so stop pretending you're a one size fits all shop. You want customers who are naturally drawn to you and your style and who will deeply appreciate what you have to offer. I've had customers send me super elaborate cake ideas they could not pay me enough to make. I just simply say: "Thanks for reaching out to me. That's a gorgeous cake, but I don't offer that style. Based on that picture I think you would love this cake that we can do for you instead." They'll usually go with my suggestion, and in the rare case that they *must* have that specific cake, I'd offer recommendations to other bakeries that I think may offer that style instead. Referrals are never a bad idea in any industry. It's a win-win because it helps the customer find what they're looking for and builds relationships with people in your industry.

Along the same lines, watch out for customers who you get that picky vibe from—the ones that will tell you where to place every last freaking detail. You *know* they're not going to like it no matter what you do (*even if* you do place every last detail exactly where they told you to). Always be kind, but be honest that you don't think you can do what they're asking and you don't feel you're the right fit for the job. More often than not, they'll recognize that they're being a little bit too particular and just tell you to do your own thing. If they keep insisting on where each detail must be placed, either get the details in writing and give them a copy so you're both clear on the outcome, or politely decline the job.

The Bad Reviews

Oh hey, 2021! You're the era of keyboard tough guys and internet bullies. Look at *them* as they type away leaving you a bad review like a maniac (just imagine their evil cackle as their negativity seeps through the keyboard). In all seriousness, there are a few reasons *why* people leave negative reviews.

Here's the most common one: they have poor communication skills.

People nowadays are substantially lacking in the social skill department thanks to social media and the internet. It's a thing. I've had people pick up their cakes (from me in person) and go on and on about how much they love it and how it was everything they'd ever hoped for only to turn around and leave a negative review about how disappointed they are with it. That's always a bit of a head scratcher. Negative reviewers often pretend to like the product upon pick up but then flame you in a review when they get home to their safety zone. It's kind of heart breaking that we live in a society that can't communicate their expectations or tell you what they're not happy with so you have the chance to fix it for them. The fact that they must resort to a negative review is sad not only for the business but for the customer too. The customer isn't getting what they ultimately wanted either. By simply communicating their wants, needs and expectations they could avoid writing a bad review and likely end up having their issues resolved, which, hopefully, creates a happy and satisfied customer (who posts a positive review).

Another reason people leave bad reviews is because they tried communicating their needs and expectations but you weren't able to help them. I hope you'd try to help resolve any issues in a kind and respectful way when brought to your attention, especially if it was your fault, but sometimes unfortunate circumstances happen that are out of your control. Maybe a customer got into a fender bender with the cake and it was ruined. While it's not your fault, they feel the need to blame *someone.* I've had a few super angry customers call to say their cake slid off its cake board and squished against the side of the box—a clear sign that they slammed on their brakes. In case you're wondering, cakes *don't* survive slammed brakes or fender benders. They also aren't capable of getting up and snuggling the side of the cake box on their own. Although it isn't my fault, I always try to empathize with the customer and offer to help them out by re-making it for them. Their anger usually fades to appreciation when they find out I genuinely care that their kid doesn't go cakeless on their birthday. This approach usually results in a positive review since it's considered going above and beyond when you fix something that isn't your fault.

This brings me to my next point on negative reviews: extraordinary customer service is the best and most effective way to prevent and negate negative reviews in the first place.

Once in a while, you will actually get a negative review that makes sense. Maybe they genuinely didn't enjoy your product or service, and you weren't able to help them. Maybe the staff member they tried complaining to was not friendly or helpful. Maybe they just didn't like the taste of your cake or the vibe of your shop. Not everyone is going to love you, and that's OK. Sometimes I get bad reviews where I think, *OK, we kind of messed that up. Even though we tried hard to fix it we just couldn't—it happens.* Don't get too worked up over the bad reviews. Encourage your loyal, happy customers to leave positive reviews and try your best to fix any bad experiences or situations when a customer is unhappy.

Also, think twice before leaving a bad review at other businesses. Ask yourself if it's something you can address with the company directly or whether it deserves a bad review. Remember, bad reviews don't actually get you what you want; clear communication *does*. If you feel the need to leave a bad review, stick to the facts and don't get carried away within the confines of your keyboard because you might just run into that person at some point—*awkward*.

Grab that notebook or loose-leaf and let's get started on the exercises.

Lesson Two Exercises:

1. Learn the difference between haters and complainers. Think back upon some negative encounters and determine if the people were haters or complainers. An easy way to decide this is to find out whether they purchased your product or not. If they did, chances are they're a complainer. If not, they're probably a hater.

2. Create policies surrounding each circumstance. A policy is a clear outline of how a situation should appropriately be handled based on the company's values. A policy for dealing with haters could be as simple as not offering a response and blocking and deleting the person from all forms of communication. A policy for dealing with a complainer could be responding to their complaint in a kind and appreciative way and providing them with a small token of appreciation like a discount toward a future order or a free product. Those are just examples, and you should come up with policies that match your brand and values and implement them so these situations don't constantly drain your energy and make you feel sad every time they happen.

3. Reflect on situations where you've dealt with difficult customers and negative reviews. Be honest with yourself and ask whether there was anything you could've done differently to prevent them from leaving the bad review. Learning from past situations is a great way to create new and improved policies and procedures that have the potential to prevent bad reviews.

4. If people leave bad reviews, either respond in a kind and professional manner offering them an incentive to change it to a positive (if possible) or don't respond at all.

REBECCA HAMILTON

Chapter Six

Lesson Three: Defining Your Values and Picking the Right People

This may sound insignificant at first, but I learned this the hard way so you don't have to! The whole motivation behind this book is for you to learn from my mistakes and get on the fast track to success. You don't even need to own a business in order for this concept to work for you in your life, but if you *do* own a business, the time to define your values is *today*.

Defining your values in everyday life will help you find and attract the right types of people into your life. The types of people you click with the most are people who share similar values as you. Of course, you can have friends in your life that have different views and perspectives on things but *values* are non-negotiable. Imagine you have values centred around integrity, honesty and trust, and you're friends with someone who cheats, steals and lies… It *wouldn't* work! I recommend clarifying and being very specific about your personal values and then transferring them to your business plan. Your business values should match and reflect your personal values.

I learned the importance of defining values at a Disney Institute business seminar a few years ago, and it really opened my eyes to how important it is. I mean, Disney obviously knows what they're doing. The thing is, whether you write down and define your values or not you *still* have them. They're either intentionally and thoughtfully created or they're just a by-product of how you go about your day. Intentionally defining them will make your life a million times easier. You'll find yourself surrounded by better friends, you'll attract a better partner, and if you own a business you'll hire better staff. If that's not incentive enough to get the ball rolling on this then I seriously don't know what is.

When you take the time to define and write down your values, you are clarifying what you stand for and, more importantly, what you do not stand for. Values are obvious in every action and decision we make regardless of whether we're aware of them or not. The more your values align with the people you hire, the customers you serve, the vendors you partner with and the organizations you support, the better your business will flow and the more successful you will be.

Because I did not clearly and intentionally define my values when starting my business, Chad and I hired *all* the wrong people in the beginning. My gosh, it was a nightmare. We hired people who weren't honest, which resulted in us firing them. We hired people who had no integrity, which resulted in them not always doing the right thing when no one was around to supervise them. We had to learn the hard way. Of course you want to trust people and not judge too harshly, but if there's one thing I've learned about people, it's that once they show you who they are, believe them! That goes for friendships, relationships, staff or anyone else in your life. If they do sketchy things or lie to you once, they'll do it again so don't naïvely hope they'll *change* because I guarantee they won't.

Here's some of my personal and business values so that you have an idea of how to start defining your own. Feel free to use some of mine if they feel right to you.

Integrity

Honesty and trust is paramount to my success in business and in life. A life anchored by integrity will be a fulfilling one, and it will be a magnet for success and endless opportunities. Integrity means always doing the right thing even when no one is around, even when it's not the *easiest* choice. Call it karma or "what goes around comes around," but girl, that shit is real. I don't believe for a second that it's possible to achieve a truly happy, fulfilled life without being anchored by integrity.

Goals

I've already mentioned how important it is to be a goal digger, but it took me awhile to fully understand the true benefits of setting goals. I've always been motivated and driven, but I wasn't always specific about my goals. Without clearly-defined goals, my constant hustling didn't always bring tangible results. If you don't have goals, girl you lost. In the woods. With no compass. No smartphone. No Starbucks. *Nothing.* And ain't nobody who wants to be stuck anywhere Starbucksless! If you don't set a goal to get out of the woods, you'll be walking in circles. *Forever.*

I set clear goals to plan the most efficient route. Then I track my progress along the way. Once your goals are set (and written down in specific detail), everything you do daily should bring you a step closer to achieving them. Keep yourself in check and ask yourself if what you're doing *daily* is inline with your goals. If it's not, either stop doing it and implement better daily routines or realign your goals.

Inspiration

Inspiration is life. Think about it: if you're not inspired to do something how do you feel when you're doing it? Yuck. Of course, there's going to be things that don't spark inspiration that still need to get done (like doing the dishes, for example, because in my industry there's a lot of them). If you're human, you probably aren't naturally inspired by doing the dishes. Now think about how you feel when you're inspired to do something. For me, it's a magical feeling of wonder and excitement. Quite the contrast. Aim to spend 80% of your day on things that inspire you and 20% on things that just simply need to get done. You will feel happier, more fulfilled and have more positive energy to crush your goals. When you're inspired, you'll inspire others.

Growth

Tony Robbins said: "If you're not growing, you're dying." Think back to when you were fourteen and imagine how different your life would be if you didn't grow and develop since that age. Yikes. You'd be walking around with your know-it-all attitude, trying to win Mother of the Year for your Tamagotchi and singing "MMMBop" into a hair brush… Or was that just me? Humans need to grow and be challenged in order to achieve greatness. We'll never reach new heights, push new boundaries or be presented with abundant opportunities by remaining stagnant. (Google the definition of stagnant; you're welcome.) Don't set up shop in your comfort zone unless you plan on being a prisoner there forever. If you're locked up there right now, it's time to get inspired, set your goals and plan your prison break.

Achievement

Girl, when you hit your goal this is called an *achievement*! Repeat that first sentence for me.

I was guilty of ignoring this for *way* too long. I had that same "OK, but what's next?" attitude. Stop it right now. Don't downplay your achievements, celebrate them. This should literally be the easiest, most fun part of your journey. If it's not, you're doing it wrong. Think about it: why do you set goals in the first place? Obviously, to *achieve* them. It sounds super obvious, but I know 98% of you skip this step the same way I used to. Naturally, as a highly-motivated person, you want to skip right to the next goal on your list. It's like skipping dinner and going right to dessert (see, if I had no integrity I would totally condone this considering the industry I'm in, but don't do it because you'll feel like shit). Listen, you're a human being with feelings and emotions; you need to *feel* things. Feel the sense of accomplishment, pride and success. Feel all the emotions that accompany achievement. Share those feelings with your friends, family and customers. Pour the red, white or whiskey and cheers to it!

Feel it. Share it. Cheers it.

OK, now you can carry on to your next goal.

Success

Do not think for a second that my definition of success should define yours (or anyone else's). Success looks so different to everyone, and you define what it looks like to you. Maybe it's a beautiful healthy family of six, maybe it's travelling the world, maybe it's the house of your dreams, maybe it's more money, maybe it's more free time… Whatever it is, be honest with yourself and what it means to you. Your dream home could be a cabin in the woods and another's could be a condo in NYC. Get clear on what success looks like to you because this is the absolute core of what's going to motivate you to keep going when things go sideways.

Write down what success means to you or—better yet—create a vision board you can see every day. Go over the top with it. The more specific, the better, because when you achieve what you have personally defined as success you'll genuinely be excited about it. Make sure to celebrate the success of all magnitudes. Don't just have the mentality of "When I make a million dollars I will feel successful." Even IF making a million dollars would make you feel successful, have gratitude throughout the journey and celebrate the smaller achievements along the way. Increasing your sales this year is ultimately one step closer to that million dollars, so celebrate it.

Gratitude

"Stop expecting and start appreciating." This quote will literally change your life.

Start practicing this daily, then teach your kids, husband, wife, staff—everyone who will listen. The world needs so much more gratitude and so much less entitlement. What are you grateful for? Write it down. Yell it out loud! Draw pictures. Whatever you have to do to acknowledge these things, do it. You'll be surprised at how long your list might be. Now try to feel bad *while* simultaneously feeling grateful at the same time. I don't know about you, but it's pretty much impossible for me. Gratitude is your best friend who will serve you well and never let you down.

Entitlement is gratitude's enemy. How many times have you felt entitled by thinking, *They should have done this*, or *I would never do that*, or *If I were them…* No. Stop it. This is the biggest, ugliest mindset mistake in the human race, and everyone is guilty of it at some point or another. Including me. It's human nature to react with those statements when people don't act how you want them to. The important thing is how you respond to yourself when you have these thoughts. The second I have one of those ugly *I wouldn't/They shouldn't* thoughts, I just *have* to poke some fun at myself starting with, *That's hilarious, Rebecca. They clearly aren't me (where's the colourful hair?). They've walked a completely different path than I, and they have different values and beliefs. It's so ridiculous that I would even think they would act like me.* Why do we feel so entitled that the way we would/should do things is the one and only way to do them? Of course you may handle situations differently, but be gracious and have a sense of empathy for where that person is coming from. When you lose the expectations and start appreciating, your life will change.

Fulfillment

While success may be linked to *some* material things, fulfillment is not a commodity. Fulfillment is the all-encompassing feeling when everything in life aligns in a way that gives us a sense of purpose or meaning. In order to feel fulfilled we need to dig deep and answer some honest questions:

- What is my purpose?
- What are my values?
- What are my beliefs?

Be specific in your definitions and notice if there are any areas you're not actively engaged in. When you're living a life aligned with your purpose, values and beliefs, you'll naturally feel fulfilled.

* * *

Defining our values is an essential step in living a fulfilled and happy life and in growing an exceptional company. Once you take the time to clearly define your values, you'll attract like-minded people who want to work with you, and you'll be able to quickly identify people who do not match your values.

Once you've defined your values, stick with them. Don't bend on them for anyone or anything. You'll run into plenty of people, employees, customers, vendors, organizations, etc. who do not share your values, but there are plenty who do. Choose the ones who do and kindly dismiss the ones who don't.

Let your values be your guiding compass in all your decision-making so they reflect the very traits of the people you hire, vendors you work with and people you do business alongside. Your values will not lead you astray.

Notebook time again.

Lesson Three Exercises:

1. Spend time honestly reflecting on your values. What are they? Write them down and write out the definition along with specific examples of what they mean to you and what it looks like when someone is emulating that value. What does it look like when someone does not emulate that value? Creating contrast between values will offer the clarity you need to quickly identify people who reflect similar values and the ones who don't.

2. Make a list of anyone in your life who does not share these values. Have you noticed you've run into conflicts with them in the past without really knowing why? Understanding that people's actions are a direct reflection of their own values can help you to understand them better. The more you surround yourself with like-minded people who share similar values, the stronger your connections will be.

REBECCA HAMILTON

Chapter Seven

Lesson Four: Fear Will Paralyze You, and Waiting Will Kill You

It's a fact. Waiting *will* kill you. Think about it: if you wait around long enough you will quite literally die. It takes less than one hundred years to prove this point (and that's *if* you're lucky enough to live a full life). Not everyone is so fortunate. Time is a precious and limited resource. Waste too much of it and that's it. Death is the literal end of your goals, your dreams and of *you*!

Are you scared yet? I hope so.

If you're not scared to death by the reality of time running out on you then you're either too comfortable to care (so why are you reading this book?) or you're *paralyzed* by your fears. Don't worry, I'm here to help you overcome your fears and tell you why waiting is killing you (and your business).

I didn't always know this stuff, and it did not come naturally to me or with any level of comfort or ease. I was so risk-averse that making big moves was extremely difficult. I was so scared of failure, which was kind of crazy because I had failed so many times. Usually when people do something often enough, they gain a certain level of comfort with it. Failure isn't exactly one of those things. It sucks every *single* time.

It took me three years of making cakes at home before I mustered up enough courage to open my first retail location. Once I finally ended up getting the guts to do that, it took me four more freaking years to open my next one. Sure, I had my "issues" or "reasons" (read: excuses) like my health was garbage and I had no energy, but even when I finally figured those things out, I still wasn't moving much faster or taking the action required to reach the lofty goals I'd set. Don't get me wrong, if my goal was to have a comfortable living and run my one small bakery, that would have been fine. Everyone's goals are different. If your goal is to have a huge family then it would be very different from my goal. But there is one thing that is fundamentally the same with *all* goals: your effort level needs to match the size of your goals.

When I was starting out with my business, my goals were *not* aligned with my effort levels. My goals were sky high and my effort levels were base level—at best. To put it bluntly, I wanted to be super successful and make lots of money while remaining cozied up in my comfort zone taking no risks and facing no fears. Had I stayed in that comfort zone I would have never achieved *any* of my goals to date. *Something* had to change. Either I needed to lower my goals to match my effort or significantly increase my effort to match my goals. Living in the middle of having high goals and the unwillingness to do the hard things is what leads to feelings of unfulfillment and unhappiness. So, if you're currently in that spot where you're not happy and not feeling fulfilled, I can pretty much guarantee it's because your goals are not aligned with the action you're willing to take to make them happen.

Be honest with yourself and look at your goals. Are you currently doing everything possible to achieve them or is your effort level shit like mine was? I'd never be writing this book had I not found the strength and courage to chase my gigantic dreams back then because I wouldn't have grown to a place where I'd be able to share my achievements with you and how I obtained them. I would've missed out on all the accomplishments, connections and friendships I've been blessed with along the way. I wouldn't have started my blog, podcast or videos either. My life would be substantially different, and to be honest I can't picture it being any different. I'm happy and fulfilled. But those feelings won't stay that way for long unless I set *new* goals so I can continue to change and grow; growth equals happiness. A lot of people strive for goals and eventually achieve them and are still left wondering why they don't magically feel fulfilled. It's because the fulfillment and happiness actually comes from the journey and growth aspect of striving to reach goals and not in the achievement of the goals themselves. The only purpose for achieving the goal is so you can set a higher goal to push you even further and help you grow so much more. Once I understood this concept, I began to pay attention to the journey and appreciate the process along the way which resulted in feelings of ultimate fulfillment and happiness.

The greater the risk, the greater the reward. Don't forget that. If you're taking baby steps toward your goals, expect to get baby-step-sized rewards. Nothing great is ever achieved by exerting minimal effort, so if you're like me and want to achieve greatness you better get your heart and soul ready for living life far far away from your comfort zone. You better get comfortable with being uncomfortable. If you want to live an extraordinary life filled with financial freedom, deep and meaningful connections, freedom to travel the world and material things that actually spark joy, you can't *be* like everyone else. Therefore, don't act like everyone else. You cannot be average and do what average people do. Average people are not bad people, they just get stuck in what society tells them is "normal" and comfortable without questioning it. They take a quick glance around and see everyone else doing average things and living average lives so they follow along. They don't question it. Even if they *think* they want to achieve all those big lofty goals, they're certainly not willing to risk their comfortable lifestyle for them.

Less risk equals less reward, which is why we can't get caught up in what our friends and family are doing or telling us that we should be doing. Chances are they're content living their average lives. As much as we'll never understand their significant need for comfort and remaining the same, they'll never understand our lust for life and achievement. I recommend you agree to disagree and let each other live the lives they choose to live. It's totally possible to live in harmony with people who aren't as driven as you are, but you *will* want to find a group of friends who are on the same journey as you. These people will "get you," and there's nothing more satisfying than sharing your journey with like-minded people who'll cheer you on and help you along the way.

If you're reading this book, you're hungry for more. You're not like the majority of our average society. You're the exception. You're different. You want more. You feel it burning in your soul. My advice? Train yourself to be so insanely uncomfortable with being average, and get uncomfortable being comfortable. Study what average people do and go out and do the opposite. Be extreme and demand results from yourself. If your average friends spend the majority of their spare time on Netflix and video games, spend yours on things that get you closer to your goals. No one cares about your goals as much as you do, and no one is going to achieve them for you. It is up to you and you alone to dig deep and find the courage, resilience and tenacity to face your fears. Look your fears dead in the eyes and tell them to fuck right off. Should that line be on a T-shirt? I think so.

What is fear? I've written a bunch about "facing" it, but what is it? Wikipedia says fear is "an emotion induced by perceived danger or threat, which causes physiological changes and ultimately behavioural changes, such as fleeing, hiding, or freezing from perceived traumatic events. Fear in human beings may occur in response to a certain stimulus occurring in the present, or in anticipation or expectation of a future threat perceived as a risk to oneself." In other words, unless you might actually die (or become seriously injured from almost actually dying) then fear is completely made up in our imagination. Ninety-nine percent of the time we're scared because of a make-believe story we've concocted in our minds that may or may not be true. The majority of made-up fears stem from one fundamental human emotion we cannot live without: love. We fear being rejected or disappointing someone. We're emotional beings, so it makes sense that our fears would stem from lack of love. But are you going to let *that* be the reason that holds you back? I sure as hell hope not!

Get *comfortable* with fear, show fear who's boss by intentionally seeking it out. Ask yourself what would scare you the absolute most right now. I'm not talking about being eye to eye with a tiger, although the song is catchy, and I don't mean something that's physically going to harm you. I mean the hundreds of other fears you're holding onto so tightly that you're allowing them to hold you back. What are they? Identify all of them. Write them down and face them one by one. We can't understand the sheer power we possess inside ourselves until we actually face our fears and conquer them. Hint: you'll unleash so much hidden potential that you'll be unrecognizable. This is one of the most powerful self-development tools you'll ever do, and it'll be the biggest gift you could ever give yourself. Just imagine all those fears you wrote down disappearing. Then what? Dig up more fears and plow through them too. You'll be unstoppable.

Now that I've let you in on the secret that fear is basically just a false perception, you *can't* unread this. You know better now. Go do better with what you know.

I'm telling you this because I have been where you are. I've experienced the intense anxiety of even acknowledging my fears out loud. I've also faced my fears and taken greater risks. You can experience similar results if you're willing to take similar levels of *risk*. I didn't start truly achieving my goals of becoming successful until I started taking much larger risks that scared the shit out of me. I told you how I opened my second location in London with six times the amount of rent as my first location and only two staff. It was cra-zy! By taking the risk and committing and figuring out the details later, it forced me to make the initial move, which is often the hardest part of risk-taking. A year and a half after we opened that location, our team grew from two to fifteen staff, and we had ironed out the majority of our procedures. Then we found ourselves in the midst of a global pandemic. COVID-19. I spent a short period of time in *panic-what-the-fucking-hell-do-we-do?* mode. Then I switched to *let's-do-anything-and-everything-possible-to-keep-our-business* mode and eventually opened our third location.

March 2020, right on the cusp of COVID-19 shutting everything down, I was fortunate enough to attend a life-changing event. The Rachel Hollis RISE conference in Toronto. Simply attending this event was one of my biggest fears. Allow me to explain. I am a huge Rachel Hollis fan. I love her books, podcasts, videos, journals, swag—everything. But, I am also an introvert. Large social events and gatherings drain me, make me extremely uncomfortable and are *not* my idea of a good time. Where are my fellow introverts at? People sometimes confuse introversion with being shy. I'm not shy. In fact, my personality is very assertive, goal-oriented and straight forward. I'm very comfortable addressing challenging situations head-on, and I don't get embarrassed easily if you need to ask me advice about personal situations (if you know what I mean). As an introvert, I just prefer more quiet events, intimate settings, less stimulating environments and small group interactions. My idea of a fun day is a hike in nature with a Starbucks in my hand followed by a relaxing bubble bath. I love to curl up on the couch next to my dogs with the fireplace crackling in the background while I read a self-development book. If that makes you cringe, you're probably an extrovert. Like Chad. Shout out to all my extrovert friends who keep life interesting.

So, the RISE Women's Conference was a *huge* stretch for me. Let's just say it didn't get me out of my bubble, it *burst my bubble*... in the best way possible. When I first heard of her event, I thought if it ever came to a city near me, I would *have* to go. How would I find the courage to do that? I didn't know. But I would have to go when and if the time ever came. Spoiler alert: the time came. Straight to my inbox. Shit. Now I was second guessing myself. I knew in my heart I wanted to go, but did I actually? I went back and forth about the idea for at least a month. It was getting annoying. Make a freakin' decision lady! I decided there was absolutely no way I couldn't go because I would feel so wimpy and deflated if I chickened out. Even if it was nauseatingly, almost painfully uncomfortable to think about. *Nobody* other than Rachel Hollis would have convinced me to attend a big city women's conference *on my own*. Oh, and it wasn't a quick little 9-5er either. Oh no. It was a three-day *stay-in-a-hotel-by-yourself-and-walk-through-the-streets-of-Toronto-alone-to-get-there* women's conference. I'd be surrounded by thousands of strangers (the kindest, most friendly and like-minded strangers, but strangers nonetheless), which was literally *terrifying*. Other people are scared of the dark or serial killers, but networking, group activities, socializing with people I didn't know and sleeping in a hotel alone were straight out of a horror film plot to me. Dramatic, I know.

I bought my ticket for the March 2020 conference on November 29, 2019. *Perfect*, I thought, *I have lots of time to muster up the courage to actually go.* My ticket was $1016.74 for the three days. I made sure to buy one of the more expensive tickets so that the business woman in me would have a better excuse to *actually* go and not chicken out. How could I forfeit a thousand bucks? Strategy is everything. Plus, I've always wondered if those conferences that cost thousands of dollars actually deliver the kind of value I expect for the price. Another spoiler alert: they *abso-freaking-lutely do!* So, March arrived. I attended. Solo. All three days, *and* I even participated fully. Just to be clear, full participation at these events meant (but was not limited to): hand holding, hugging, dancing, jumping, crying and talking about vulnerable, difficult things with complete strangers.

It. Was. Freaking. *Life-Changing.*

Not only because I had just conquered a *major fear* and overcome *several* fears I had surrounding the conference, but because of all the invaluable tools I learned. I had no idea just *how* impactful it had been until all the knowledge and skills I'd been taught were be put to the COVID-19 test. The whole world shut down a few days after I returned from this conference. Chad was even supposed to leave for a four-day Tony Robbins conference in California two days after I returned, but it was cancelled. So, it was totally meant to be for me to be there, and I got to attend it just in the nick of time. It not only helped me through COVID-19, but it assisted me in making the best decisions during this insanely scary and challenging year. This was one investment in myself that paid off big time, so if you're not sure if those conferences or self-development books actually work, try one out. They do work *if* you take the action after you gain the knowledge. So grateful for you, Rach. Facing this fear allowed me the opportunity to learn the key pieces of knowledge that I didn't even know I'd needed to make it my best year yet and to truly *thrive*.

COVID-19 was about to teach us another valuable lesson: how to pivot. Luckily we'd always kept our business up to date and current, so we already had a functioning website where people were able to order our products online and have them delivered locally or they could select an option to pick up their order in our store. I can't imagine any businesses who were behind on having a website and offering online ordering because it would've been a substantial factor in making it through this challenging time since everything switched to online, delivery and curbside pick up. We saw where things were headed and immediately pivoted to match the increased demand for delivery since people were too afraid to leave their homes. This was when we decided to purchase a fleet of delivery vehicles. That's right, when most people were scaling down, we were scaling up. I wasn't sure if it was the smartest or the stupidest thing I'd ever done, but in the name of keeping my business alive, I was about to find out. Chad and I worked non-stop through the lockdowns doing anything and everything humanly possible to keep shit going strong. And it worked. We were growing at a substantial rate, and it was growth we would've never had if we didn't take the risk to purchase the delivery vans. It was so scary spending that kind of money in such uncertain times. No risk, no reward—remember?

Shortly after that major purchase we decided to take another gigantic risk by opening our third location in Woodstock. Right in the middle of the freaking pandemic. This was *really* about to be the stupidest decision or the smartest. We chose this location because many of the deliveries we were now making were going there. Naturally, we followed where our customers were at and opened up shop. It's been a huge success right from the start.

Taking such great risks in short periods of time proved that moving quickly in the direction of my goals was the path to truly achieving them and becoming successful. Now that I know this, I can't unknow it, and I hope you'll take this key lesson on your journey to pursuing greatness. This was 2020, the year that wreaked havoc on our health-care system and society and paralyzed people with fear. It was the year I realized if I wasn't willing to take massive risks and pivot to adapt to the changing circumstances daily, my business would have been *destroyed*. It would have succumbed to the wrath of COVID-19 like many other small businesses that didn't make it. 2020 was the year we doubled our sales from $600,000 to over one million.

Open that notebook again, and let's apply these lessons.

Lesson Four Exercises:

1. Make a list of all your fears. Make sure they're actual fears and not just things you sort of don't like doing. They should make you want to puke because the thought of doing them scares you that much.

    For every fear, write three things you're going to do to overcome them.

    Do them and check the fears off your list one by one. It's not going to be easy, but it'll be worth it, and it's the quickest path to success.

2. Have you taken any risks? If so, what were they? How could they have been bigger?

    Make a list of much larger/riskier things and write three ways in which you will tackle them.

3. How have you invested in yourself lately? Write a list of new ways you plan to invest in yourself and be sure to do them. They always pay off!

Chapter Eight

Lesson Five: If You Don't Want to Quit, You're Doing It Wrong

Holy shit. I almost quit a billion and twenty-five times! That's a lot… It's also a pretty specific number that I totally made up, but it certainly felt like I wanted to quit *that* many times. Let's just say there was no shortage of "situations" that pushed me to the brink of fuck this shit. Whether you're just starting a business, thinking of starting a business or currently running a business, let me offer a teeny tiny bit of advice: *expect* shit to hit the fan. If you expect it to happen and it doesn't, you can enjoy a great day while it lasts because tomorrow is a new day of shit-might-hit-the-fan potential! Seriously, just know that issues are going to happen at the worst *possible* time. If you accept that that's how it works, then when it *happens* you won't be so shocked. Issues happen at the *worst* possible times. Expect them. You're welcome.

This book would legit be way too long if I started listing off every single challenge I've faced and issue that arose. The truth is, we *need* to hit those walls because they are what we ultimately stand on top of to boost us to new heights in our businesses. The struggles are what challenge us and test how far we're willing to take our business. Business is hard. It's going to push you, pull you, tear you apart and break you, but it will also build you up stronger than you'd ever imagined you could be. So if you don't want to quit a million times over, you're doing it wrong. You either don't *care* enough or you're not working *hard* enough.

My hope is that you fantasize about obtaining a "regular" 9-5 job often. Why? Because you'd never actually go back to your comfy old 9-5er. You'd never do it, but if the idea of it brings you brief comfort, it means you're facing challenges in your business. That's a great thing. Entrepreneurs are built for challenges and overcoming breaking points that average people aren't able to handle. We're wired differently. In fact, as much as we hate to admit it, I think we secretly love the thrill of being pushed to the brink and coming out on top stronger than we were before.

The best entrepreneurs are *always* the ones who've struggled the most. They're the ones who come from a rough childhood or overcame some kind of trauma. Many of the most successful people in the world have their own compelling stories of rough pasts that have built them and prepared them to handle and overcome anything life throws their way. When you've experienced rock bottom all the other challenges in life are more like inconveniences. When you've been through something traumatic—like trying to find the comfiest way to rest your head on cold concrete for the night—your threshold for daily issues and inconveniences is so much higher. An angry customer doesn't affect you when you've overcome larger obstacles and tougher hurdles. If someone who hasn't dealt with significant challenges in their life spills coffee on themselves on their way to work, it will probably ruin their day because they aren't as resilient. I'm not saying you *can't* be an entrepreneur if you haven't been through hard shit, but going through hard shit certainly gives entrepreneurs the *advantage*. If you compare an entrepreneur who has had a relatively easy life, great childhood and no significant trauma to an entrepreneur whose experienced the opposite, the person who has overcome the most pain will overcome business challenges more easily. If you've never been through anything worse than what you're currently experiencing, then it's going to seem so much more challenging. Make sense?

I didn't have a good childhood. My dad had severe anger issues, and my mom justified them. There was swearing, name-calling, thrown plates shattered against walls, false promises, overturned furniture and occasionally some sore skin. There's no other way to put it—it was the worst time of my life. I never felt safe or in control, and love was something you earned via "good behaviour" and/or "keeping quiet."

Even as a child I knew my dad's anger was irrational because he would make a huge deal out of things I'd never seen any other adults get that upset over. Such as a misplaced TV remote. If it wasn't exactly where he'd left it, you'd better hope you weren't the one he thought watched TV last. It was so confusing as a child because I'd been at friends' houses, and their parents would laugh and joke about who lost the TV remote. It would even turn into a cute little family game of who could find it first.

Kids are much smarter than people recognize; I was. I had a hard time experiencing joy and excitement (even later in life) because expressing it was "irritating" and "unacceptable" unless Dad was in a good mood at that exact time. Eventually, I stopped feeling joy and excitement altogether because there was always the threat of whatever was provoking the joy to be taken away based on his mood. There were countless times where we'd be on our way somewhere, it didn't matter where, and if anything remotely pissed him off, he'd literally turn the car around until my mom would beg him to stop acting so irrationally. It took *nothing* to set him off. Everyone walked on eggshells around him at all times. If the house wasn't clean and dinner wasn't ready, my two younger brothers and I would immediately flee to our rooms. No way did we want to be in his path when he arrived home to a "lived in" house and dinner "still in the oven and not ready" because that would surely result in thrown plates—or worse—thrown toys that left trails of our broken treasures in his wake.

Fast forward to my teenage years and, as you can imagine, the PTSD of such a rough childhood had taken its toll on my fragile and developing adolescent mind. I'd had enough. If you think teenagers are emotional under normal circumstances, well let me tell you. Everything I'd witnessed growing up was a recipe for fucking disaster. I was fuelled by anger, resentment and anxiety, and I had lost all respect for my parents—my dad for the obvious, and my mom for not doing anything about it. In short, I was done being the scared little girl, and my fear turned into rage. It was the only prominent emotion I'd ever known to be acceptable in my family, so it came naturally. I was always on edge, ready at any given moment for a screaming match. It usually started with my parents having an argument with each other, which I would no longer be able to contain my (very unwelcomed) opinion on. It didn't matter if I was defending my mom, my brothers or myself, it always resulted in a screaming match of epic proportions. Not exactly the most mature response on my part, but it was all I knew at the time. It got so bad that my parents didn't know what to do with *me* anymore since I'd always find my opinion front and centre of their senseless arguments.

That's right, they labelled me as the problem. Forget the fact that their arguments involved screaming, throwing objects and name-calling. Right. It must have been *me* since I was the only one standing up for what I thought was obscene behaviour that I thought adults were able to control.

"Are you on drugs?" my dad once asked me, implying that I must be out of my mind to be so angry and resentful toward them.

For the record, I'd never touched an illegal drug in my life. Their idea of solving the problem was to get rid of me. They discussed checking me into a shelter but, luckily, my aunt offered to take me in for a few weeks so they could have a break from me. I didn't care; I loved my aunt. She always acted as though she understood me, something I really needed at that point in my life. I thoroughly enjoyed time spent away from my home and from refereeing my parents' stupid arguments. It was them that needed a break from each other, permanently. Eventually I had to go back home, and nothing ever changed because *no one* ever changed. My parents frequently kicked me out of the house, and I was forced to stay at friends' places, sketchy motels, random friends of friends' places and boyfriends' places. I even spent nights on the street. The incredibly sad part was that anywhere else was better than "home."

One can only take so much of the instability of being kicked out of your home on a regular basis, so I decided to move out with my boyfriend. I was sixteen. I dropped out of high school, and the struggle was definitely real back then. I was young, lost and on my own. Obviously, I wasn't capable of having great relationships with boyfriends because, well, the example I had set the bar pretty low. I flip-flopped from breaking up with boyfriends and living on my own, to moving in with the next boyfriend and craving the love and normalcy I'd only ever witnessed in relationships on TV. I'd experienced abusive relationships that I thought were normal, and I often resorted to thoughts of suicide for comfort. It was an awfully hard time, and I found myself in too many what-the-fuck? situations. While my friends worried about what to wear to high school dances or who they were going to invite to sleepovers, I was worried about budgeting my money strategically so I'd avoid running out of groceries again. When you're a kid trying to navigate the harsh reality of the world alone and dealing with adult problems, it's a dangerous and scary place to be physically, mentally and especially emotionally. I recently came across a meme on Facebook that said something along the lines of "When I look back to when I was younger, I wonder how the hell I'm still alive." Yep. That's me. I moved around frequently and found myself working at a local adult fun store, if you can believe it. I sold things from lingerie, sex toys and novelty bachelorette items to things I will absolutely *not* mention in this book. I mean, it certainly was an *interesting* job to say the least, but not exactly where I had hoped to end up permanently. So, when people like to reminisce about the good old days, they can count me out… The good old days for me are *today*!

I'm not sharing this story to tell you how awful my parents are. They just didn't know any better, and to be honest they probably *did* a better job raising me than their parents did with them. They obviously learned their behaviour from somewhere. So, I think having empathy for people and where they came from is really important. I shared my story to paint an honest picture of where I've been and the challenges I've had to overcome to get to where I am today and to show the beauty that came from it. I've been to therapy and healed significantly through my willingness and desire to become a better person. I hold no grudges toward my parents and feel like I finally hold love and empathy for them. As my mom likes to say, "We did the best we could." I hated that saying with a passion until I actually took the time to understand what she meant by it. For years, I totally thought they could've and should've done better. I understand now that if someone isn't able to see there's a problem they can't fix it. With that understanding, I believe they actually did do the best they could. They didn't know any other way and weren't at a place within themselves to get the help they desperately needed. You don't know what you don't know. Adding kids into the mix of their already tumultuous relationship couldn't have been easy.

I've forgiven them because forgiveness is part of *my* journey and has nothing to do with them. You might be surprised to learn that I actually hold so much gratitude in my heart for my parents, my past and all the struggles I faced so early on. How? Because I *know* they're the reason I developed the resilience, grit and tenacity that shaped me into the boss woman I am today. I wholeheartedly believe that the pain and trauma I endured in my past armed me with the strength to achieve greatness. If you've experienced some kind of pain or childhood trauma, consider searching for the help you need to heal from it and don't let it define who you are today. The difference between the scared child you once were and the person you are today is that you're an adult now, and that means you're in full control of your life and destiny. It's so easy to continue to feel sorry for ourselves and stay stuck in the replay of the traumatic events, but nothing great will rise from that. Please heal your past wounds via professional help so you can experience the true beauty and freedom of finally being responsible for how the rest of your life plays out. We get to decide if we're going to stay a victim forever or if we'll rise from the ashes of our past and use the tough lessons to propel us into the life of our absolute dreams.

Some people assume successful people were born that way. They don't see everything they've had to go through to get to that point. In order to experience the highest of highs, we need to have experienced the lowest of lows. So, it's no wonder that I'm able to handle the stressful situations like a champ that other people might find difficult. Finding the motivation and desire to simply choose to live another day was stressful to me, so minor inconveniences like a spilled coffee, a messed up cake or customer complaints are easier stressors in comparison.

I hope that opening up and sharing my story helps you find the positives in challenges you've faced. Don't get caught up in whether your story is better or worse than mine, but look for the lessons you've learned and how your past shaped you into the person you are today. If you've experienced trauma that you've yet to heal from and still feel sensitive about, please reach out to a therapist and get the help you need to heal and live your best life. Don't spend any more time on this earth suffering from past pain; life is precious and beautiful if you decide for it to be.

Those Fucking Chocolate Pretzels

Let me tell you about those fucking chocolate pretzels. Back when I opened my first location, I was so focused on sales and taking as many orders as possible (as you do when you open a brick and mortar location with *real* rent to pay) that I had absolutely no concept of time management—and I do mean *no* concept. Little did I know, I was about to be taught a very valuable lesson about it.

I was just getting started on my last order of the day in the late afternoon. I was tired from an extremely busy week but found a second wind of enthusiasm and excitement because all I had left to do for the day was decorate some bride-and-groom-themed chocolate pretzels for a wedding the next day. The only problem? There were 350 of them. I clearly didn't realize the amount of time it was going to take to complete *that* many hand-decorated pretzels. Away I went. I dipped. I decorated. I packaged. *What the hell?* I remember thinking, *Why are there so many pretzels left?* I felt like I'd already done a million by that point.

Luckily, Chad had just finished work at his day job so he stepped in to help. Even between the two of us, it was like we weren't making *any* progress. These were clearly more tedious and time consuming than I had expected… We dipped. We decorated. We packaged. The best comparison I can relate it to was Mary Poppins never-ending bag—you know, where she just keeps pulling out objects after objects and you're like, *Where the hell are they all coming from?* It was like a sick magic trick where for every one pretzel we dipped, ten more appeared in its place. We ended up ordering dinner in from the great Thai restaurant across the street because there was no way we'd make it home for even a late dinner by that point. We took a quick dinner break and went back to it.

My hands were sore, my feet hurt, I was absolutely exhausted. All of a sudden it was 3:00 a.m. and we *still* weren't nearing completion.

"I literally can't do this anymore," I told Chad as tears began pouring down my face.

He encouraged me to take a break as he could sense my irritability and frustration, so I did. I took a break alright. In the corner, on the un-mopped, sticky floor amid the chunks of salt and smudges of chocolate that had fallen. I bawled my tired eyes out into my chocolate-dipped hands. I was having a complete meltdown (is that a chocolate pun? I think it is). It was *too* much. This business was *too* much. I felt like I was such a failure, and I just wanted to *sleep*. Chad kept dipping away while trying to comfort me. I remember telling him I didn't think I could do this business anymore.

"Why don't you go home to bed and get some sleep, I'll finish the pretzels," he said.

Although the offer was kind, being the perfectionist I was, there was no way I was letting him finish decorating these pretzels because the bride expected them to be *perfect*. No offence to Chad, but he's a banker not a decorator. I pulled myself together and generated enough drive to push through the rest of the night, puffy strained eyes and all. We ended up finishing up around 6:00 a.m. Yep, we pulled an all-nighter, but we got them done and they were perfect.

The true hero of this story is Chad, who went to deliver them to the wedding venue in the morning (which was basically right after we'd dipped and packaged the last pretzel). He then returned to run the storefront after being up for twenty-four hours while

I went home to rest. What a guy! The moral of this story? Fuck chocolate pretzels. Also, you'll be pushed past your limits many times in business and be forced to find the strength to finish the job. True business owners find that strength and do *whatever* it takes. Giving up is not an option when customers are relying on you. This story reminds me of a great quote I heard recently: "I didn't come this far *only* to come this far."

I haven't dipped a chocolate pretzel since.

My First Wedding Cake

Here's another one for you. The first wedding cake I ever did was a four-tier square white fondant cake with black damask and pink ribbon—the trend of the year way back. Half of it was made up of Styrofoam and the other half actual cake. If you're a cake decorator, please don't do these cakes. The Styrofoam is basically the same price as real cake, and it takes the same amount of time to decorate it. If you're going to use fake tiers of cake, at least make sure you charge the same price you normally would. I wish I had known this back then but nonetheless, this bride was cheap and I was desperate, which is never a solid foundation for doing business.

I had done large, tiered cakes for parties before, and surprisingly the party cakes were much more time consuming and elaborate compared to wedding cakes, but the fact that it was for someone's *actual* wedding made me nervous. I worked so hard and put all my heart and soul into this cake. Chad drove the unassembled cake and me to the wedding venue where I would be assembling it on-site to ensure it wasn't ruined during transportation. I was so nervous of all the venue staff who had gathered around watching my every move while tiering this cake. They seemed to find it fascinating, while I was on the brink of a heart attack. Shout out to all my cake decorators who can relate!

Finally, the cake was assembled, and I was incredibly proud of how great it had turned out. The fondant was smooth, the damask was perfect and—most importantly—the cake was level. The staff were all asking for business cards as they marvelled at the cake. I felt the biggest sense of relief and was glad that it was over and I could carry on to enjoy my day.

A couple hours later and... *Ring, ring, ring...* Chad answered. It was the groom. I could hear him yelling and swearing on the other line as a huge pit formed in my stomach. I was so confused. *What is wrong with the cake?* I racked my brain for any of the possible reasons they may be unhappy about, but I just couldn't come up with any. Which was *rare* because if there was anything that was easy for me to do it was to pick apart imperfections and deeply criticize my own work (after all, artists are the most critical of their own work).

"The bride hates the cake," Chad said after he put the groom on hold.

I was shocked.

"Well, ask them why and what they're unhappy with," I said. "I can go back and fix anything they want."

You'd think an offer like that would have turned the whole thing around. Nope. The hostility continued. If they weren't able to communicate what was wrong and allow me to fix it then what else was I supposed to do?

"We want our money back," the groom declared.

Aha... the truth comes out. They didn't hate the cake or want anything fixed, they wanted a *free* cake. I hate it when people prey on other people's insecurities and try to benefit from it. I wasn't prepared to refund their cake simply because they wanted a free cake. What kind of policy is that? I really didn't know what to do with someone who couldn't tell me what they didn't like or allow me to fix it. Who goes through the theatrics of calling on their wedding day to complain and try to get their money back? It was so bizarre. I knew I had to offer them something, so I suggested a free cake for their anniversary the following year or for any other occasion. They weren't super thrilled with my offer but the call eventually ended.

A couple of days later, I got a couple of bad reviews from the groom and the bride (yes, they left separate reviews so that I got two negative stars instead of one. How thoughtful). The reviews stated how awful the cake was and how everyone hated it and that they deserved a full refund. I can't say I didn't see it coming, but what I didn't expect (and I couldn't even make this up if I tried) was when I clicked on the bride's profile picture—I shit you not—it was a picture of her and her fiancé cutting the freaking cake on their wedding day. Yep, the cake I poured my heart and soul into that they said they hated. Gosh, for someone that hated their cake so much it was kind of weird that it made it into her profile picture! Am I right? What the actual fuck though.

Yes, there will be those who try to take advantage of you, but people are generally good. Try not to let one negative experience ruin your confidence and all the positive experiences you've had. It's far too easy to focus on the one measly negative review even when there's been a hundred positive ones. Resist the urge. Ask yourself what you could learn from the negative experience or do differently next time, and move on. Do not let it fester inside or define you. You can expect to be pushed to your breaking point often. In fact, if you're not, then (you guessed it) you're doing it wrong.

Always Have a Backup Plan

Now that I've been running my business for a while and experienced all kinds of challenges, I've learned the importance of a backup plan. If I show up to a wedding venue and their cake is quite literally in shambles with crumbs all over the trunk of my car, I make sure I've got enough time and product back at my store to fix it. I was not always so well-prepared though, and I've had my fair share of cake mishaps. Luckily, I'm an extremely solution-based person and always think of how I can fix the situation. I don't let my emotions get in the way or cloud my ability to problem-solve.

I also always make the decision in the best interest of the customer and not in my *own* best interest. For example, if it's 5:00 p.m. on a Saturday and the wedding cake doesn't make it to the venue in one piece, I'm prepared to get to work and make a brand new one and deliver it in time for cake-cutting pictures and dessert regardless of what I'd planned after work that day. As much as I'd love to be done for the weekend, I couldn't live with myself knowing I didn't fulfill my obligation to a bride on the most important day of her life. I've had to miss my own events, reschedule appointments and work longer than I'd planned on several occasions, but my integrity always outweighs my own wants. I suggest you adopt the same level of integrity in your own business. It is imperative to your reputation. Always have a backup plan.

Even though I've said "Fuck this shit" out loud more times than I'd like to admit, I never truly meant it. When my head says, *Screw it*, my heart always steps in to say, *Stop being a whiny little bitch*. Literally. My heart and soul are so invested in my business, that quitting is never an option. It's a fantasy at times, but a real, viable option? Absolutely not. Whomever came up with the saying "It's a piece of cake" (which implies that cake making is easy) can fuck right off.

Time to put this into practise.

Lesson Five Exercises:

1. Did you experience a traumatic childhood? Write about it and how you feel about it now. Do you notice that you still hold significant pain and unforgiveness when you talk about it? If so, write down the actions you're going to take to start your healing journey. It might involve journaling about it or seeking professional help from a therapist. Make sure you have a strategy to help you heal and take control of your future so you can start living your best life.

2. What is your plan for handling adversity in your business or life? Write down five types of adversity that have happened in the past year in your business or life.

   Then evaluate on a scale of 1 to 10 (1 being the worst where you were not proud of how you handled it and 10 being the best).

   Ask yourself what you can do differently if a similar situation arises. It's important to reflect on our shortcomings and ask ourselves the tough questions in order to improve our response to difficult situations next time.

3. Write down five worst-case scenarios that could arise in your business.

   For each scenario, write down three great solutions you can resort to if one of those things happens. For example, I would write down: a wedding cake falling apart during transportation to the venue. Solutions would be:

   a. Make sure I always stock extra cakes and supplies in case I need to re-make it.

b. Make sure I deliver to the venue at an early enough time in case I need to re-make it.

c. If a cake is over two tiers tall, I will assemble it on site to avoid any damage to larger cakes.

Having a game plan will help you when you're involved in the stressful situation!

Chapter Nine

Lesson Six: It Is ALL of Your Business

Have you been told your whole life to "Mind your own business" or "That's none of your business"? Guess what, lady? If you have a business, it's *all* of your business! Oh yes, that includes the sales, staff, culture, marketing, branding, products, policies, expense sheets, taxes—the whole damn thing is *all of your business*. Don't confuse this with you having to *do* it all, but you're responsible for the implementation and oversight of it all. Don't give that power to anyone else unless you sell your business (for millions, of course).

It's true. In order to scale and grow your business you'll need to hire staff to work in key areas to get the jobs done and keep it running smoothly. But don't think that means you can just leave it be, head out to Bora Bora and get drunk on piña coladas. Oh no, you better be prepared to monitor it closely. The overall success of your business comes down to *you* as the entrepreneur and the level of awareness you have for what's going on.

Here's my top eight areas of business that you *must* pay attention to in order to grow a successful business.

1. Sales

Sales trump everything. If you don't have sales you do not *have* a business. If your business is struggling, it's because you don't have sales. Sales are more important than top-of-the-line equipment, a great business plan, the design and layout of your store, web design or the colour of your business cards. It's easy to get caught up in all those other things because running a business is fun and dynamic and there's so many areas to shift your attention to. But don't get distracted and don't take anyone else's advice if they're telling you that sales aren't the absolute most important part of your business. Sales are *everything*. If you let other things distract you, you will be out of business before you know it.

OK, Rebecca, we get it! Sales are key, but how do we get sales? Glad you asked.

Sales are simply you exchanging a product or service that people *need* for money. Make sure the product or service you're selling solves some kind of problem for your customers. Tell them how and why it'll make their lives better by buying it. Show them why they absolutely *need* to have it in their lives. Grant Cardone says it best in his book called *Sell or Be Sold*: "You're either selling to someone or they're selling you their excuses as to why they won't buy it." Think of all the reasons people come up with to not buy your product and then create great counter offers to their excuses.

Money and sales come from people because people are the creatures that carry the currency. So, the more people you surround yourself with, the more potential buyers you'll have. One important thing a lot of people miss when it comes to sales is, don't sell *to* people, sell *for* people. The more you genuinely care about the people you're selling to, the easier you'll be able to explain the benefits they'll experience from what you're selling. The best sales are made upon building genuine connections and relationships since that's what will ultimately lead to lifetime buyers. The more authentic you are, the more long-term sales you'll get.

Always always always follow up in all situations. If you didn't get the sale, follow up with the customer to see if they're still interested or why they haven't bought yet. If they did buy your product or service, follow up with them after to see how they liked it. Yes, it might seem uncomfortable to open yourself to feedback, but it's truly important and the most valuable way to learn how to improve. When it comes to sales, you don't get what you don't ask for. If you truly believe in your brand or product, you'll feel like it's a *disservice* to anyone who doesn't buy it.

2. Marketing and Building Your Brand

You can have the best product in the world, but if no one knows about it, guess what? It doesn't matter. Businesses with the best marketing and brand presence always outperform and make more money than businesses that have the best products. *Always.*

The word "marketing" can be intimidating, but you'll need to harness its power. It simply means connecting with your customers on a human level that they can relate to. The same way you'd initially attract a life partner: by being the best version of yourself, being overly kind and attentive to their needs/wants and giving them your undivided attention. It's *so* basic. Create content that resonates with your audience. People are hungry for human connection now more than ever, so feed them with your content (and cake).

Take a look at your values and come up with creative ways to incorporate them into your marketing efforts so you attract customers who share similar values. Those are the people who will stand behind your business. Marketing is all about creating feelings and emotions and drawing people closer to your product, service and business. The more they relate to you on a human level, the more they will buy your products and spread the word about your business. Think of all your favourite brands and ask yourself how they make you feel. Branding is all about *feelings*. The best brands know how to touch us on an emotional level and create an inseparable bond between them and their customers.

Using "social proof" has been a very successful strategy for me. I mean, it makes sense in today's society where we're so consumed by social media and glued to screens that allow us to see highlight reels of what our friends are doing, loving and posting about. There's a reason "influencer" is now considered a viable career: influencing *actually* works. When people see other people that they admire or relate to enjoying a product that appears to be making them happy, they want it too. In other words, when people see pictures of their friends who are obsessed with your products, they will feel like they're missing out on something epic. I focused on creating the most colourful, whimsical and Instagram-worthy products so that when people saw their friends posting photos with our treats, they just *had to* have them too! It works.

3. Customer Experience

If there's any area of your business to be over-the-top and "extra" with it's in the customer experience department. Be genuine, authentic and at their service. Customer experience is what differentiates businesses within the same industry. Chick Boss Cake might be one of fifty businesses that make great cakes, but my customer experience and the genuine relationships I've built with my customers helps me stand above my competition. Try your absolute best to make anything and everything happen for them, and think of creative ways to exceed their expectations in ways that they'd never imagine. Always aim to over-deliver. Don't just meet expectations, exceed them. There's many ways to do this like a bonus gift, exceptional service or going out of your way somehow to make it a memorable experience for them.

Customers expect to receive a certain level of customer service, but they'll become fans and tell all their friends and family about you when you go over and above their expectations. Ultimately what you want is other happy customers selling *for* you because you gave them something to rave about.

The bar for customer experience is set so low nowadays that simple common courtesies such as a free cupcake when they book a custom order in store, opening the door when they enter or leave, bringing their items to their car for them or engaging and entertaining their kids so they can peacefully look at the menu will stand out. These are a few things we do to try to show we truly care and are so grateful they decided to spend their time and money with us when they could be *anywhere* else.

To what lengths will you go to show customers how grateful you are and how much they mean to you? I mean, I feel like we do it naturally when it comes to intimate relationships or even friendships, but customers should be *no* different. Especially if you're looking to grow your business to a million dollars in sales.

4. Policies, Procedures and Systems

I know, I know. This part royally sucks, but if you want to run a successful business, you need to get shit out of your head and onto paper. That means *everything*. You need a policy for all areas, a code of conduct and a procedure for how to properly complete all tasks because employees need structure and clarity. They may not like it, but they desperately need it.

This is a critical part of the growth and development process.

Make everything extremely easy to follow and understand. We have a step-by-step system for every single aspect of our business because customers expect consistency and this is the only way to achieve it. We have everything clearly outlined with how to properly bake our products, how to decorate them, how to clean up, how to package orders, how to do deliveries, how to wash the dishes, how to act professionally at work, how to approach customer service, how long each task should take to complete, how to handle complaints—everything.

All functions of the business are written down and easily accessible on our company tablets that we use for our daily operations. Our team can look anything up quickly, so they know the expectations and how to complete all tasks up to our standards. Each employee has a tablet to use throughout their shift with all the available information they need to know each day including a detailed schedule to follow. When they come to work, they grab a tablet and pull up their Time Management schedule, which is a spreadsheet of tasks to be completed in chronological order. Each task is accompanied by an allotted amount of time per task and they are expected to complete their schedules each day. If you don't use technology to run your daily operations, an old-fashioned binder with printed documents will do the job. Make sure the expectations are always clear and that you hold everyone accountable.

Start organizing all your systems, policies and procedures now and create clear, easy-to-read documents for your team to access at all times. By creating clear-cut policies, procedures and systems, you're not solely relying on the expertise of any one single employee (who could potentially quit tomorrow). Instead, you've got systems in place and can train and hire new people quickly with consistency each and every time!

5. Expenses

You do not need top-of-the-line equipment when starting out. In fact, if you spend money on top-of-the-line equipment starting out, you'll be out of business before you know it. Invest in only what you need starting out and be as minimalistic as possible—trust me on this. It's so tempting to buy the fancy shelving or shiny new store displays, but you know what? That shit doesn't *actually* make you any money! Get second-hand stuff and get creative. You should spend your money on things that will *actually* make you money such as marketing, products and inventory.

I started my million-dollar bakery with $5000 of someone else's money (a business grant I received from the local business development centre). For entertainment purposes, I should mention that the board who approved my grant came to the consensus that my business would *not* be successful. In the feedback of my approval letter, they wrote something along the lines of how they approve the majority of businesses for this grant and that was basically the only reason for my approval. They straight-up told me they were fairly certain my cake business would fail. They clearly didn't know who they were talking to. I can't help but chuckle about their thoughts as they've watched my business grow into the million-dollar bakery it is today. Thus, the importance of not listening to the haters (or anyone for that matter) telling you that you can't do *anything*.

Anyway, I used that 5k toward my first month's rent and to buy the bare minimum of necessities. I used a small, crappy consumer-grade Kitchen Aid mixer and regular residential ovens. Why? Because they worked. Obviously they weren't the most efficient tools since they only produced small batches, but they were all I needed at the time. Saving money on those tools allowed me to spend money on advertising to bring in new customers so I could afford to grow and expand. It's way too easy to get consumed with the thoughts of needing all the high end commercial equipment—you *do not* need it. When you prove your business to be successful and profitable and have the stability of sales beneath you, then you can *slowly* upgrade.

Use your money wisely and be extremely creative in the beginning. Only spend money on things that you either actually *need* to operate or that make you *money* in return.

6. Personal Debt = Bad. Business Debt = Good

Personal debt is bad because it doesn't make you money. Business debt is good because it will actually make you money—if you're smart! If you plan on getting to one million in sales, you'll need to stop fearing debt. Successful businesses need capital to be able to scale and grow. There is no other way. The problem with this concept is that most of us have been wired to think that debt is this awful and terrible thing that you do not want to have. While that is true in situations like personal credit card debt accumulated via shopping sprees at Kate Spade, not all debt is the same and not all of it is bad either.

Think about your mortgage, for example. It's not necessarily bad debt because owning a home is an investment. The word investment is just a fancier word for debt. So if that word makes you more comfortable, then consider any debt you incur to help your business grow and become more efficient as an *investment*.

As mentioned above, only spend money on things that will make you money in return. Obviously, there will be things here and there that you'll want to renovate, touch-up or make prettier as time goes on, but do not go into debt to do those things. They will *not* make you money. Look, I'm all for a pretty, Pinterest-worthy space, but like I've said before, get creative and do not invest a lot of money into cosmetics until you have excess money coming in. You'll *need* to invest money directly into your business in order to substantially grow.

You'll know the time is right to upgrade once you've done the following:

- Ironed out the details of your business;
- Created operational systems;
- Hired staff to help you grow;
- Proven that customers love your product;
- Achieved stable sales throughout all seasons.

Anything you invest in needs to either make your back end more efficient thus resulting in labour savings or help you on the front end like adding another location that will generate additional revenue and pay back that debt and then some.

7. Products

You know the saying "Less is more"? This applies to the quantity of products you carry. You need to know that *quantity* of different product options is not the key to growing your business and increasing your sales. In fact, having too many products is confusing to people, and confused people will not buy from you.

I made this mistake in the beginning since I had no idea what I was doing. I thought that the key to growing and expanding Chick Boss Cake was by growing and expanding my product line. Hell no. In the beginning, I'd do all kinds of things from cake pops, candy apples, cookies, eclairs—literally everything. I was a jack of all trades but master of none. The different products required so many different ingredients to keep in stock, and there was no way to make the baking process more efficient. Keep your product line minimal in the beginning and streamline your processes for efficiency. Focus on becoming the best in your industry with the limited items you offer, and expand your product line slowly, one product at a time.

Also, if you're starting or growing a business in an artistic industry, you need to be extremely careful of the products you're making. If you want to scale and make millions then it needs to be easy to train staff on making your products. I definitely learned this the hard way. When I started out I was making all kinds of crazy and cool 3D elaborate cakes myself. I loved it, and I was pretty good at it, but I quickly realized I wouldn't be able to train anyone else to make these types of cakes since it was really an art. All artists have signature styles. Imagine if Picasso tried training painters to recreate his paintings in a similar style. I mean it just doesn't work like that. I notice this issue within my industry often. A lot of very talented cake decorators manifest these elaborate cakes they'll never be able to train anyone else to do the way they can. It's not scalable. Perhaps they just want to make a decent living, which is great, but if you want to scale you'll need staff to be able to reproduce your products in an efficient and consistent way.

I eventually stopped doing those elaborate cake designs and created a "signature style" of cake with candy and fun edible decorations exploding at the seams. It represents my style and artistic flair while still being easy for staff to recreate in a timely and profitable manner. The best part about creating a signature style of cake designs is that they become super recognizable at parties and in pictures. Like, "Oh look! They got a Chick Boss Cake for their event!"

8. Staff

Nothing is more crucial to the growth of your business than having a great team. If you want to grow your business to a million in sales like I did, then prepare to step up your staff game. When I began writing this paragraph on staff, I noticed it was getting quite lengthy, so I'm dedicating the entire next chapter to the topic.

In the meantime, let's take a look at some exercises to cement this knowledge.

Lesson Six Exercises:

1. Write down the eight key areas above and ask yourself if you're actively overseeing them to the best of your abilities. If some don't apply yet, write them down anyway so you can come back to them later. It's important to know the key areas to always keep your eye on, but if you're too actively involved in one area I suggest you hire someone else to fill that role so you can focus on the oversight of all these areas without getting overwhelmed.

2. Circle the areas that your business is currently doing exceptionally well and highlight the ones that aren't up to snuff yet. Having a clear visual is important, so make sure you focus attention on the weaker areas.

Write down three ways you can improve each of the weaker areas starting right now.

REBECCA HAMILTON

Chapter Ten

Lesson Seven: The Staff Struggle Is Real

What the actual hell! You mean to tell me that it's not enough to simply *pay* people money and they'll *actually* just do their job? How dare they be so entitled, needy, demanding and unmotivated. Aren't they grateful that I've busted my ass to build this business to the point where I've created employment opportunities for them? Don't they know that if the business fails tomorrow they'll be out of a job?

As you may have sensed, I don't get why employees don't care the same way *I* do and why they aren't motivated to help me take this business to the top. I know my fellow business owners with employees can relate. Hiring staff is frustrating and expensive. See, when you work so hard in your business to make money and you're grinding away, it's painful to pay someone to do a job you could do better yourself. Whenever there is money involved, there are always expectations attached to it.

Does any of this resonate with you? It's all too familiar to me because these were my exact thoughts for years. Hiring was—by far—the biggest challenge of growing our business, and it seemed completely hopeless. Here's a secret for you though: you don't get to a million in sales *without* staff. So, I think it's safe to say that we've come a long, long way in figuring out the best, most effective management strategies.

I can sense the eagerness for you to read this chapter because I know for certain that if you're an entrepreneur or business owner, you'll struggle with staff! How can I say that with such certainty? Easy, because your mindset and motives are literally the *opposite* of an employee's mindset and motives. Understanding this is the key to unlocking all the secrets to employee happiness, productivity and retention.

Ask any business owner who is actively trying to grow and scale their business what the #1 pain point is for them. They'll tell you (with intense frustration and hopelessness) that it's the staff.

News freaking flash my friend: it's not the staff—it's *you*.

Before you hit send on any hate mail, allow me to explain. I totally agree with your feelings—they're real. I still have them. Here's the deal though: If you don't work through those feelings and develop a strategy for coping with them, you'll never have any staff. Either you'll get frustrated and fire them or they'll get frustrated and quit. *Neither* of those situations get you closer to a million bucks.

So, let's agree that staff can be super challenging, but they also hold the key to your growth and ultimately the success of your business. So, set your ego aside and listen closely to what I'm about to tell you: Staff are the most important component in growing and scaling your business. They're also the hardest part of growing and scaling your business.

Your Management Style

There's nothing more complex than managing a team of different personalities who all have different skill sets and require different management styles. A great manager does not have a set management style but adapts to meet the individual needs of each employee. The worst managers are the ones who blanket manage employees based on their own personal beliefs of what a manager "should" do and "should" be. The best managers I worked for prior to starting my own business treated me like an individual and met me where I was at. The worst ones managed me like I was a robot—everyone was managed the same way.

We can't manage everyone the same way because everyone is not the same. Humans have unique needs and wants and bring different skills, insecurities and issues to the workplace. There is no effective way to blanket manage individual human beings. We just can't. Now, don't get this confused with the fact that it is our job to set the standards and be consistent in managing those standards. If we have zero tolerance for a bad attitude, we better be prepared to correct this behaviour every single time it shows up. Being a great leader means that we clearly communicate the expectations and step in to address any issues that are not inline with them.

So, if its Monday afternoon and you've got a full list of tasks to do, but you notice Emily's negative attitude, it's your job to step in to immediately address the issue and ensure she understands your expectation going forward. It's easier to overlook bad behaviour when you're busy or aren't in the mood to deal with it, but the long-term impact of letting your expectations slide will have serious consequences for you (and your team) later. Always stay true to the standards you set, even when you don't have time.

Not Everyone Is Meant for Management

It's important to know your own strengths because not everyone is *meant* to be a manager. For example, I am *not* a manager. It is *not* my strength. In fact, it's probably one of my biggest weaknesses. I have a CEO mindset, and my skill is to create, invent, make money and oversee operations. I am an extremely driven individual, and while I am fully aware of the importance and art of managing people, I am not the person for the job. So, I don't pretend to be. However, I do understand the key components on how to effectively manage. I recommend you learn the skills to effectively manage so you'll know what to look for and how to train a manager effectively when you're ready to hire one. Chad is a great manager and has really developed the art and skill of leading our team.

An entrepreneur or business owner mindset is: how can I grow, cultivate more sales, build a better business and conquer the freaking world? An employee mindset is: what's for dinner tonight, I'm kind of pissed off at my boyfriend so I need some time with my friends, maybe I'll text Jess on my break to see if she can meet up after work. See the difference? The employee comes to work to make a *living* so they can create a comfortable and enjoyable life for themselves, and an entrepreneur is trying to take over the world and is willing to do whatever it takes to do that. If you don't have a manager to bridge that gap between the two vastly different mindsets, then it's up to you as the business owner to develop the appropriate managerial skills in the meantime because somebody's got to do it. Just like any other skill you've learned and developed in order to operate your business, managing is a skill that must also be honed. Pay close attention to this chapter.

Always Listen, Communicate and Give Them What They Say They Need

Always be the "bigger person." You're the business owner and the one with the expansive mindset, so you need to see life through your employees' eyes; don't expect it to be the other way around or you'll be in trouble. The more you try to wrestle employees onto the same page as you, the less they'll feel understood and the less connected they'll feel to you and your business. This is definitely not what you want.

Understand that *anything* they tell you is their own truth. If they're extremely stressed out with life, it's not up to you to compare their level of stress to that of your own. I understand that it might seem silly that their life could be remotely stressful *especially* when comparing it to your own where you have greater responsibilities, but it's not a comparison game. No one is trying to out-stress each other here. The sooner and more clearly you can see their struggles from their perspective, the more understood they'll feel.

If Paula comes to you and tells you she needs fewer shifts because working full-time is too much for her right now, I'd recommend accommodating it. It doesn't matter if you wouldn't be stressed out by working forty hours a week—after all, you probably work significantly more than that—the point is that forty hours is too much for her to handle, so give her fewer shifts. What's it matter to you? You pay her hourly anyways, so hire someone else to fill the gaps.

It's awkward and challenging enough for employees to even discuss their issues with you, so the last thing they need is for you to make them feel bad or insignificant for feeling a certain way. Take their feelings seriously and make as many adjustments as needed to help them feel better. Employees who feel understood generally end up being better employees who work harder.

It doesn't stop there—why would it? *Expect* their minds and circumstances to change on a regular basis because employees generally haven't learned how to manage and stabilize their moods and will often allow their frame of mind to dictate their level of happiness and ability to perform. What stresses them out this week might not next week or a month from now, so commit to open communication and accommodating their ever-changing needs. It is imperative.

Oh, and don't expect them to come to you first because most employees are intimidated by their boss and find it easier to just get a whole new job than to address issues in their current one. Which sounds ridiculous, I know. I find this especially common in the younger generation who grew up glued to screens; their ability to confront issues and communicate their needs is a real-life challenge to them.

It takes time and costs money, but if you want your employees to stay and help grow your business, treat them like an investment and not a short-term commodity. If you listen and give them what they tell you they need, you have a better chance of retaining long-term staff, gaining their respect and keeping them happy. Happiness equals productivity.

You may be thinking, *What the actual fuck, Rebecca? How am I supposed to run my business by giving them everything they want?*

To which I would reply: *Well, Susan, how are you supposed to run your business with no staff?* It is super important to cater to their individual needs as much as possible so that when the time comes to drop the hammer or say no to something, they will respect you because you have their back nine times out of ten. Also, when you have to say no, it helps if you explain to them why you're unable to fulfill their request this time and assure them that you appreciate everything they do. There is no substitute for clear and open communication. People just want to feel loved, so if you lead with love, you'll get love in return. There are things you're in control of and things you aren't, as I will point out next.

But What If They Want to Have Their Cake and Eat It Too?

Yes, it's true that sometimes they will want things that they're not willing to work for. After all, they don't always know how the real world works, especially if they're fresh out of school. If an employee expresses interest in a raise or a promotion, you need to clearly outline the next level of responsibility, expectations and what they need to improve to be considered for that role. I encourage my employees to ask for promotions and raises, but they know they'd better come prepared with a list of extra responsibilities in exchange for that ask. Effective negotiation and asking for a raise is a great skill to develop that they will use for the rest of their lives, so it benefits them as well. If that role requires a significant number of hours and the employee who is inquiring about it needs every other day off, be honest about their current limitation and tell them it's not going to be the right fit. Let them know that if their situation changes, you'd be happy to consider them at that time.

Giving employees what they want does *not* mean compromising your business and giving them more responsibility when they're not capable of handling it. It sets them up to fail and will not only make them feel worse, it will jeopardize your business. Putting them in roles where they'll succeed and thrive based on their own capabilities is win-win for both of you. Promotions are earned, and employees should always be excelling in their current role before being considered for future advancement. You're in control of what you pay them, what they need to do in order to get a raise, what promotions they're eligible for and what positions you promote them to. Simply put, you're in full control of your business and how you run it; you're not in control of the limitations the employees put on themselves.

On the flipside of this, just because someone is performing well in their current role does not automatically make them a great candidate for a promotion. I employ some really amazing staff who crush it in their current job and, naturally, I want to promote them, but they don't necessarily want the added responsibility.

Unless someone expresses interest in moving up, making more money or getting a promotion, let them keep crushing their current job. They may be doing an exceptional job because they genuinely enjoy doing it every day. If you push them to take on more responsibility in a different role, they could lose that spark and job satisfaction. Employees are happiest when they're thriving and doing what they're good at. It can be tempting to try and help them grow into different roles, especially if they're your best employee, but avoid this. Not everyone has the same drive and ambition that you do, and just because you would appreciate the promotion and new opportunities does not mean they would. My best advice is to communicate the opportunities for growth often so they know they exist but emphasize it is up to them to tell you if they want to pursue them. Oftentimes, employees simply want to know there are plenty of opportunities for growth within the company even though they don't always wish to actively pursue them. It is just the comfort of knowing.

While I care deeply about people in general and I thoroughly enjoy implementing fun and creative ways for employees to enjoy their jobs and love coming to work, I'm not the one to patiently sit down and tend to their unique, fluctuating moods and needs. Which is exactly what you need to do as a manager. Chad is fantastic at this and has honed his management skills significantly. He's patient, encouraging, helpful, meets people where they're at, is able to adapt his level of communication to many different personalities and identifies when a situation requires disciplinary action and when to let it slide. I, on the other hand, assume that if I've told you something *once* you'll magically "get it" and remember it forever and ever, amen. At least I'm self-aware enough to know how ridiculous that sounds and that I'm not a natural-born manager. Delegating someone in your business who has the soft skills to implement the important management strategies is essential to the long-term growth and well-being of your business.

Focus on your strengths and hire other skilled people to fill the roles of your weaknesses.

Manage Staff like You're the Coach of a Winning Sports Team

You're the coach and the employees are your players, which means you're the one in charge of orchestrating the team in a way that sets you up to win! It's imperative that you ensure that the operations of your business aren't hindered by the fluctuations of your players. That means you need to know who your key players are (your starters) and have enough players on the bench to fill in when needed.

In business terms, you're in control of how many hours you delegate and to whom you delegate them to. If you want to create a winning business you need to give your key players (a.k.a. your best employees) as much time in the game as possible. By doing this, you're also setting the standard that your weaker players should aspire to if they want to receive more shifts. Creating friendly and healthy competition among your team is the best way to set a higher standard and give everyone a solid benchmark of what's expected in order to be given more shifts. Business is not a charity, and I don't believe in operating it like one, so if an employee wants more shifts or preferred hours, they need to be the best worker with the best attitude. Period. I realize that seniority is a common workplace benchmark, but I honestly don't give a shit about seniority unless the person with the most is legitimately the best worker. Don't get me wrong, I value the loyalty that accompanies seniority, but if it also reeks of entitlement and complacency, then forget it! It's useless. If you're going to manage your staff like the coach of a winning sports team, make sure you let them know the rules of the game before they start playing so they know what metrics you'll be looking out for.

Also, you're in control of how many people you hire. Always be hiring and in search of new talent. Yes, even when you don't think you need any more staff. There's two reasons:

1. You could be passing up the next best employee simply because you didn't think you needed to hire at the time that they happened to apply.

2. You never really know when people are going to quit, and you want to make sure that you're not left out to dry. It's your responsibility to ensure you have more than enough people at all times to be able to fill in for other employees' sick time, vacation days and if they decide to quit with no notice.

Policies and Procedures Are the Winning Combo

Set your staff up for success with clear expectations, policies and procedures. Don't just assume they know how to act professionally or conduct themselves in a way that you deem acceptable. If you leave this to chance, you'll find big trouble! The more clearly you outline their job duties and expectations, the better. Staff feel more comfortable when they know what is expected and how they can succeed at their jobs. If you have no policies or procedures for how you want them to do their job then they'll just do what *they* think they should, which is a clear path to disaster and a huge communication error on your part. I guarantee their way is not the most efficient or cost-effective way to do things because they're not the business owner. Doing things their way usually means whatever way is easiest for *them* and gets the job done so they can go hang out with their friends.

If you clearly document everything in your policies and procedures from what they should wear, how they should act, examples of acceptable behaviour and non-acceptable behaviour, how they will be evaluated and what the disciplinary action process is, you're on the right path. Even things that seem like common sense must be documented—trust me on this. I've had to train staff on how to respectfully resign from a job with the proper two weeks' notice so they leave on good terms and with the opportunity for a great reference. This training came after witnessing a string of staff throwing temper tantrums and quitting mid-shift for something not going their way. It became apparent that no one had taught them how to respectfully and professionally resign or told them what the consequences that can accompany such immature and irresponsible decisions can be. Naturally, you'd expect people to know how to resign in a professional way, but I've learned to not assume anyone knows anything and just cover all my bases. As much as staff don't love rules, they actually hate lack of clarity more. Once you've defined all your systems, policies and procedures, be prepared to lead by example and follow them yourself. Nothing pisses off other people more than being told to follow rules by a leader who doesn't follow them as well.

Ensure all their tasks are broken up into their simplest forms, and eliminate multitasking as much as possible. Just because *you've* had to multitask in order to grow and scale your business does not mean that employees will be any good at it. In fact, multitasking can be quite costly since it is usually where mistakes happen. Humans aren't great multitaskers by nature, so the easier you make the job the better. Structuring your business this way will result in quicker training times when you hire, fewer mistakes and overall happier employees.

Don't Be the Parent, Be the Cool Aunt

I don't have kids, but I think of managing staff as parenting except you're the cool aunt or uncle that the kid *sort of* likes. This concept applies regardless of the average age of employees. I'm just using this as an example of how to properly handle your role as an authority figure to anyone below you. Whenever there's a sense of authority above, the people below will naturally look for ways to rebel and disagree to a certain extent. Similar to children. Yes, you want to be the adult in charge if you're the manager, but you also want to be an authority figure that they feel comfortable turning to if they need help. If you're managing a team, assume the role of the cool aunt/uncle where you love them like they're your own, show them tough love when needed, let them break a few rules when Mom's not around but step in to tell them when they've crossed the line and implement disciplinary action when needed. Listen to their problems as if you genuinely understand them, and send them back home to their families at the end of the day.

My aunt was all of those things to me, and it's why I felt comfortable talking to her about things I'd never talk to my parents about. Parents almost always have hidden motives when it comes to their kids because they want their child to make "smart" and "good" decisions instead of watching them stumble or fail miserably through making their own. Their concern usually comes from a place of love, but that doesn't necessarily make the kid feel like their feelings are understood. Ultimately, it's the lack of understanding between the authority figure and the people below them that creates misunderstandings, resentment and friction. The better you're able to bridge that gap and communicate to people on whatever level they're at, the more successful you'll be at managing your team.

You Need Them, They Don't Need You

Check your ego at the door because if you don't agree with this yet you'll want to pay very close attention here.

If you plan on building your business to one million in sales or beyond, you'll *need* staff. Don't be naïve enough to think you can do it all on your own. You cannot. The best way to hire the right people is to clearly define your company values and find people who match those values. Do not underestimate the importance of hiring people to fit your company values and culture. Make sure their work environment is fun and reflects things that are important to them. I want my staff to have access to things I *know* to be important for mental and physical health (whether they choose to use them or not is up to them, but I personally feel better knowing they have access to them). Providing them with things that are beneficial to their health and well-being in combination with things they genuinely find appealing is the perfect mix for developing a great work environment. You want to inspire them to grow and expand their horizons but also provide them with perks that they value at their current level.

That's why I developed an Employee Wellness Package that blends both of these elements. The package includes:

- a free snack station at work;
- an allowance for books;
- an allowance for a wellness activity of their choice;
- a free gym membership;
- a paid day off and a free birthday cake on their birthday;
- a 40% discount on all our products;
- free coffee and cupcakes during shifts.

Sounds like a pretty freaking epic place to work, doesn't it? Build an environment for your staff, not for you. If you incorporate fun perks and luxuries that *they* think are cool and that their friends don't get in their workplaces, word will spread quickly and all of a sudden you'll have a line-up of people who will want to work for you. Create a work environment that makes them happy to come to every day. One that makes it *more* fun to wake up and go to work than to call in and skip work to have more fun at home. If they have more fun *at* work than they do at home, then you've done something right. Also, they'll be more productive because if they're smart, they won't want to lose their job that comes with all these unique and awesome perks!

Not sure where to start? Simply ask your employees what will make them happy, productive and thoroughly impact the quality of their daily lives. Ask them what you can do to make their work environment more fun. Listen to the conversations they have with each other. What are they passionate about? What do they talk about when you ask them about their weekend? These are all valuable ways to seek insight into what is meaningful and important to them. You need them. They don't need you. Don't let your ego convince you otherwise.

Nail Down Your Hiring Process and Don't Be Desperate

The simpler you can make the hiring process, the better. You need to know what you are and—more importantly—are not looking for. Do not give anyone the benefit of the doubt when hiring. You want to be as judgemental and particular as possible… something we're taught in kindergarten that is *mean* and *wrong*. While in everyday life being judgemental can be mean, in business it can be the difference between keeping or firing an employee and all the expenses that go along with it. People show you who they are if you ask the right questions and pay close attention to their answers. Write down what your deal breakers are and don't bend them for anything. It's easy to overlook things when someone seems like they have all the skills you're seeking except for that one red flag. Pay attention to that. If it's the negative way they talk about their old boss or they speak negatively about past situations or people they've worked for, chances are they have a negative outlook on life. Positive people will always find the positives in situations and wouldn't perceive their boss to be a terrible person even if their old boss wasn't their favourite.

Pay attention to everything they're saying and save yourself the aggravation. It only takes a few times of learning this the hard way to know exactly what I'm talking about. Every single person we've ever fired ended up waving visible red flags when we looked back on their interview or how they conducted themselves in their three-month probationary period. It's been a costly lesson we've learned more than once. Chad and I have gotten much better about not turning a blind eye to anything in the interview process (or thereafter) that may result in unfavourable situations down the line. New hires need to match your current culture, so if they don't, it's a recipe for disaster. Do not put your current team's happiness and well-being at risk by bringing in someone who doesn't share the same values.

Also, never, ever hire out of desperation. This is the absolute worst thing you could do because you'll overlook way too many red flags simply because you need someone stat. Make sure your hiring process includes a consistent hiring strategy like once every month or every couple of months so that you're hiring the best people for the job. Get to know your average turnover rate and don't let employee turnover frustrate you. Some industries have higher turnover rates than others, and to be honest, I'd rather have an employee quit than have someone who isn't productive or adding value stick around for years. It's true that training is expensive, but so is complacency.

Lesson Seven Exercises:

If you currently employ staff (if not, skip to the option below):

1. Who is currently managing your staff? Are they the right person for the job? If not, hire an actual manager or work on developing this skill yourself. If you don't, then be prepared to dish out endless amounts of cash for the extremely high turnover you're about to experience.

2. What is your company culture like? Whether you think you have one or not, you do, it's just a matter of how intentional it is. What is the morale of your employees? Take a look around and even ask them what they think the company culture is like. Then, write down what your ideal company culture would look like. It's great if you can involve your team in the brainstorming process, but you can also Google ideas that other companies have done to improve their company culture and use some of those. This should be fun, but make sure you involve your team so they don't feel left out. Employees sometimes have a difficult time with changes regardless if they're positive or not, so make it a fun and easy transition for them.

3. It's great if you can appoint one or two of your employees to be the team leader of the company culture and ensure it is upheld at all times. If you simply just write it down but no one enforces it then it'll never change.

4. What benefits do you offer? Take a look at your employee demographic to establish what they value. If they're older maybe they value the traditional medical benefits. If they're younger they might not care about traditional benefits and instead would appreciate staff lunches, snack stations and gym memberships. Knowing what your employees actually want and value should be at the forefront of your

benefit packages. Get creative and treat it like the valuable investment that it is. Happy and healthy employees always perform better and stay longer.

5. Do you have clear expectations, policies and procedures laid out in detail for them? If not, don't wait any longer to do this. It is essential to the operation of your business and to their success as an employee. Do this now. The more specific the better.

6. Take a look at your hiring process. Streamline it to be as simple a process as possible. For example, we:

- Post an ad on a hiring job board and social media;

- Review resumes and look for a couple of key qualifications;

- Send out application questions to those who match the qualifications;

- Offer phone interviews to anyone who fills out the application questions to our standards;

- Pass or fail them on the phone interview. If they pass, they get an in person hands-on interview;

- During the hands-on interview they have to follow specific recipes or instructions to demonstrate their ability to complete tasks properly. If they pass the hands-on interview we ask to call their references;

- Check their references if they seem like a good fit. Use the last two jobs listed on their resume and not just the ones they're eager to give you.

Write out your process so that hiring will be super easy because you've created a system to use. If this sounds like a lot of work, it's nothing in comparison to hiring the wrong people who are extremely costly to train and could potentially wreak havoc on your company culture resulting in great employees quitting as well.

If you do not currently employ staff:

1. Do you need staff right now? Is there an area in your business that you could use the extra help? Write down any areas that could save you time that you could pay someone else to do. Don't be afraid to pay people. You cannot build an empire on your own. Once you start delegating tasks to other people, you'll have the free time to focus on sales and other key components of your business.

2. Before you hire any staff, write down all the areas you've identified where you could hire someone else to help you right now. Clearly outline what their job duties look like and the relevant policies and procedures. If you do this step before you actually hire, you'll be able to hire a better person for the job since you know exactly whom you're looking for. It also sets them up for success since they know exactly what's expected of them and what they'll be signing up for by accepting the job.

3. Figure out what your hiring process looks like. Make this process as simple as possible. For example, we:

- Post an ad on a hiring job board and social media;

- Review resumes and look for a couple of key qualifications;

- Send out application questions to those who match the qualifications;

- Offer phone interviews to anyone who fills out the application questions to our standards;

- Pass or fail them on the phone interview. If they pass, they get an in person hands-on interview;

- During the hands-on interview they have to follow specific recipes or instructions to demonstrate their ability to complete tasks properly. If they pass the hands-on interview we ask to call their references;

- Check their references if they seem like a good fit. Use the last two jobs listed on their resume and not just the ones they're eager to give you.

Write out your process so that hiring will be super easy because you've created a system to use. If this sounds like a lot of work, it's nothing in comparison to hiring the wrong people who are extremely costly to train and could potentially wreak havoc on your company culture resulting in great employees quitting as well.

4. What benefits or perks will you offer? A discount on your products, free lunch every month, a gym membership? It doesn't have to be excessive or super expensive when you're starting out, but you do want to offer them something so they feel excited about and valued for working at your company. They could work anywhere, and every other company comes with their own set of benefits and perks.

5. Who will manage the staff? Obviously it might be you if you're just looking to hire your first few employees, so make sure you thoroughly read and understand my chapter on staff or else you'll have a hell of a time. Until you can afford to hire a manager, remember to understand the needs of your employees and take this as an opportunity to learn the characteristics of a great manager so that when you eventually hire one down the line, you'll know what to look for.

6. Since you don't have staff yet, it's a great time to plan what you want your ideal company culture to look like. Should it be fun and loud or quiet and calm? Get specific and make sure you have ways to implement the culture throughout your policies and procedures. You'll be able to find better people who match your culture if you define it before hiring them.

The Million Dollar Bakery

Chapter Eleven

Lesson Eight: Confidence Isn't Just Key, It's Everything

If you don't believe in yourself, no one else will. Confidence is a skill to be learned, practised and improved upon. If you don't have confidence, let's get to work. Like, *now*!

Most issues people come to me with can be traced back to a lack of confidence. If you work on developing and mastering the art of confidence, you'll have *fewer* issues in business and in life. Don't get me wrong, you'll still have issues, just fewer of them.

Don't feel smart enough?

Don't know what you're doing?

Do you fear your competition?

Are you scared of what people might think?

Afraid to fail?

Seeking advice from the wrong people?

These are signs you're lacking confidence, which will prevent you from achieving great success. But you can literally figure anything out.

You Can Literally Figure Anything Out

Confidence is simply your belief and trust in your own abilities. It does not mean you have *all* of the answers for everything, but that you can rely on yourself to figure them out. Being persistent in figuring things out is the best way to build confidence. Curiosity and tenacious effort will reaffirm your belief that you have the power to find the answers. The longer you stay in a state of helplessness where you don't know the answers without taking action and figuring them out the less confident you'll be.

I developed significant confidence from relying solely on myself at a very young age when I learned that the only person I could completely trust and rely on was myself. It taught me that if I didn't know what to do, I had to figure it out. Feeling out of control and helpless only wastes time you could spend finding a solution. Wallowing in a state of "not knowing" strips you of your confidence, so the quicker you transition to "I'll figure this shit out," the sooner you'll experience a confidence boost. I've had to make my own decisions my entire life, and I may not have always made the "right" ones, but I've learned from the wrong decisions and made *other* decisions to readjust. Another confidence builder. When we make a bad decision, it's just an opportunity to make the right one.

For some royally fucked up reason, women in particular struggle with confidence more than men. Society teaches us to play small and remain insecure for fear that if there were a higher population of *confident* women, they'd rule the world! If more women tapped into their unlimited potential and armed themselves with unwavering confidence, the world would change. For the better. That's why I'm so passionate and focused on helping women create the lives of their dreams and stop letting shit hold them back. A confident woman is *unstoppable*. Let's look at a bunch of statements women commonly use that lack confidence.

I Don't Know What I'm Doing

Glad you feel this way. It would be fucking weird if you *did* actually know what you're doing. The only way anyone truly knows what they're doing is if they've *done it* before. If you've built a successful business before then you wouldn't say you don't know what you're doing because you do, in fact, know what you're doing. See what I mean? No one knows what they're doing when they do it for the first time so this statement doesn't make sense. It's fundamentally stupid, but I can relate to it. I let my lack of knowledge hold me back my entire life. It was easy to convince me that I didn't know what I was doing considering I dropped out of high school and moved out on my own at sixteen—choices society deems an intelligent person shouldn't make. Realizing that no one actually knows what they're doing (even though it may appear that they do) was life changing. As soon as I quashed this excuse, I became unstoppable.

I'm Not as Good as Her

Intimidation is when we perceive someone is better or above us, and it makes us feel insecure and less confident. It actually has nothing to do with the other person and everything to do with how low your confidence is. We're better together, just like the Jack Johnson song says. Collaboration over competition is key. Stop comparing yourself to other people and start admiring their talents and success instead of letting them make you feel insecure.

Insecure people feel bad when they see others succeed or obtain things they want. Jealousy, hate, insecurity and secretly hoping others fail are all signs that you lack confidence. I encourage you to challenge these feelings, unpack the insecurities when they arise and change them into positive statements like, "Wow, what an amazing woman! I love that she's achieved so much success." Heck, even reach out to the people who make you feel insecure and tell them how much you admire them and wish them well. If you strike up a friendship with people you'd typically be jealous of and get to know them on a human level, you might learn you have more in common with them than you think.

When you're insecure and jealous, you're coming from a place of lack. Success does not and will not reside in that place. It is a weak, dark, lonely place that unsuccessful people dwell in. Let me tell you a little secret: I've cheered on and collaborated with many other bakeries/people within my industry. Does it look like my sales suffered because of it? Not one million dollars of a second! In fact, I ordered my birthday dessert from another local baker on my thirty-third birthday. It was a bunch of gluten-free doughnuts stacked in the shape of a birthday cake. Obviously, being a successful baker and cake decorator, I could've easily just made my own, but I wanted to support someone else's business and give them the credit for such a fun birthday cake idea. I reached out to this sweet and talented lady and not only was she thrilled that I wanted to order my birthday cake from her, but she refused to let me pay for it and even delivered it to my door *on* my birthday for free. Now, if that's not the best all-around heart-warming story of women supporting women I don't know what is.

It gets even better.

I posted many videos and pictures of the dessert, gave her shout-outs and talked about how much I loved it. I also recommended that my customers support her and follow her page, hoping it would result in many new customers for her. Guess what my online sales ended up being on the same day? The best daily online sales I'd ever had (at that point): $7,952.57 when the average day was about $3000. That's right, $8000 of sales in one day—more than double. Talk about a great birthday present! My point is that my business did not suffer one bit from promoting someone else's bakery. In fact, I love that I may have inspired entrepreneurs in similar industries to support each other because I showed they won't magically lose customers *or* business. I knew she'd benefit from me doing that, and that I wouldn't suffer because of it.

Someone said: "Dimming someone else's light will not make yours shine brighter." I love that and couldn't agree more.

I'm Not Smart Enough

Where the hell did you get the idea that you're not smart enough? Probably from our obsessive society where if you didn't attend an ivy league school you're basically a moron. Maybe your parents were assholes and told you this. Maybe it was a teacher, ex-boyfriend or a so-called friend. I never felt smart enough, and everyone I knew confirmed my beliefs. I hated school because my learning style was literally backwards from the way our education system likes to teach. To this day, when I'm faced with a problem, Chad and I will come up with the same or similar solutions but my way is usually backwards in comparison to his. He reaches solutions in the more "normal" way that our public education system taught him. Who the hell cares how you get there? It's so unfortunate that our education system is so biased toward learning in the traditional way that it will not work for a lot of people. Think of all the kids who are left out of that equation—mostly the creative individuals like myself. Our brains are wired so differently that it's hard for teachers or parents to understand our thought process. Of course when you're younger you just chalk it up to not being smart enough, but looking back it was every single adult that didn't think I was smart enough who were *actually* the uneducated ones. A great teacher or leader is one who can adapt their teaching style to match the unique needs of each individual person, *not* the other way around.

Let me tell you a story about how I knew it was officially over with my boyfriend whom I'd moved out with at sixteen. We'd been off-again on-again for like three years, as you do at sixteen... There were too many issues to list and so many reasons to go our separate ways, but for some annoying reason we'd always end up getting back together. Not this time. I can't remember what we were fighting about, but I do remember we were out for dinner at Montana's and he eventually called me stupid. That was it. Never talked to him again. I wonder if he still thinks I'm stupid...

No one else defines your level of intelligence other than you. You're in charge of how much and how often you learn. There's literally no excuse for you to feel like you're not smart enough with the insane amount of free information you can find online. As Tony Robbins would say: "It's not a lack of resources, it's a lack of resourcefulness." In other words, you're the only one holding yourself back.

You do not need a formal education to build a million-dollar business because you can learn from the most reputable school called life, just the way I did. Tuition is free and results are guaranteed.

I'm Scared of What They Will Think

First of all, who the hell are "They" and why are you giving them the power to control your destiny? True confidence comes from not being phased by what others think. I know it's difficult to put this into action because as humans our fundamental core need is to be loved; we innately care about whether others love us or not. This takes work to overcome. Rewiring our primal, caveman-like brains to negate natural instincts and adapt to a new, more practical way of being takes serious dedication. I've beat this by constantly reassuring myself that I know in my heart what is best for me. It also helps if you offer unbiased love, support and open-mindedness toward others who may be afraid of what you might think of them. Practising this over and over again is crucial to adopting a new belief of not caring what others will think.

I also surround myself with people who are open-minded and supportive and who don't desperately need to seek approval from others to feel validated. Don't underestimate the value of being around like-minded people. They'll fill your instinctual need to feel loved and provide you with a judgement-free zone where you can be yourself. It takes incredible courage and strength to follow a path that may disappoint your parents, old friends or anyone in your life who thinks you should be doing life *their* way. My advice: keep finding the strength and courage until it becomes second nature to not care what others think.

But What If I Fail?

You *will* fail. I'm not going to candy-coat it for you. You *absolutely* will fail at times. If you expect to fail, you can also prepare yourself for how you'll recover from it and get the hell back up stronger and more determined than before. So if the question is no longer "What if I fail" but "What if I succeed?" you put the focus on success. Seriously—what if you *actually* succeed? Focus on success and expect to fail. It's pretty simple.

Fear of failure is the *exact* thing that prevents the next great artist from inspiring you, the next great invention that improves the quality of your life, the next cure for cancer, the next Taylor Swift, the next great *anything*. Fear of failure is selfish. Plain and simple. It is selfish because you're afraid of what failure means for *you*, *your* family, *your* ego and *your* life. I encourage you to think beyond yourself and find purpose in what starting your business or sharing your talents with the world means for everyone else. Will your products help someone, solve a problem, make them happier, create a memory for them they'll cherish forever? My bakery does this. Had I been so selfishly consumed by my fear of failure, thousands of customers wouldn't have been touched by my stories, experienced my unique flavour combinations, been inspired by my creativity or made it a Friday night family tradition.

If you're afraid to fail then you're thinking too small and you're only thinking of yourself. In that case, you're not ready to start or expand your business because you need to have a purpose beyond yourself in order to create massive success and fulfillment.

Beware of Whom You Seek Advice From

Reaching out for advice and help is one of the *most* important things you can do in life and business. Learning from people who are *better* than you at something gives you the opportunity to fast-track your way to becoming a better person and growing your business. But—and this is a huge but—this can also go horribly wrong and lead you down a path that sends you further away from your goals if you're not careful! You need to be responsible for doing your research, asking the right questions and making sure the advice you're getting is from someone who is *ahead* of you or *further* along in their journey than you are. Don't blindly go asking for tips and advice from people without finding out if they're the right person to be giving that advice.

Basically, open your freaking eyes and take a look at *whom* you're asking for advice from!

I'm shocked by how many people blindly trust other people for advice on topics that clearly that person is not an expert in. Nothing pisses me off more than personal trainers who aren't in shape themselves or life coaches who don't have their lives together. Be careful. Just because someone identifies themselves as an "expert" in an area does not mean they are. Beware of people who pretend to be further along than you, and instead seek out people who are living proof of where you want to be. How much further ahead are they than you in the area you're asking them for advice on? Only slightly? If that's the case you can expect to only get *slightly* further ahead. Are they significantly further ahead of you? Then you should expect to get *significantly* further ahead (provided you actually take their advice).

The people you seek advice from don't have to be Harvard graduates, and, in fact, book-smart advice is not usually the best advice anyways. Seeking help to meet your goals in life is actually *so* simple. Look for people who are where you want to be. Look for people who have the things you want to have. If you want to have a successful business, look for people who *actually* have a successful business! Don't just get advice from someone who calls themselves a Business Advisor. Go to someone who is living proof that their business is what you'd consider to be successful.

OK, you get that you need to be asking the *right* people—the ones who are living proof of what you want to achieve. What if they don't offer business advisory services? Chances are they probably don't offer traditional "coaching" or "business advice," but people *love* helping people. It's just human nature. Stop being intimidated by their level of success, be bold and ask them how they did it so you can do it too. If the first person you ask says no then go to the *next* person. Don't give up just because the first successful person you asked was too busy to chat (successful people *are* busy people after all). You won't get the answers you're looking for unless you're persistent in seeking them out. Stop wasting your time, go right to the source to get your answers, implement their strategies and watch your life actually change.

Remember that free advice is just that—free advice. If you want legit advice from someone you admire who may not offer traditional coaching then make sure you have something to offer. After all, the successful person is taking time away from growing their own business to help you with yours, so offer them something in exchange for their time. It could be as simple as, "Can I pay you $100 to thoroughly answer five questions I need advice on?" Or offer them your products in exchange for their time. They'll take you much more seriously if you're willing to invest in their advice and show your appreciation for it.

People Pleasing

Nothing screams "lack of confidence" quite like the awful habit of people pleasing—when you prioritize other people's needs and wants above your own. I don't have a whole lot to say on this topic other than stop *doing* it. People pleasers don't succeed. The word itself quite literally makes no sense because it's impossible to please all people. If you've created a habit of pleasing people, you're setting yourself up for failure and a healthy serving of disappointment. Instead, learn to be a kind, generous and intentional person who makes decisions based on feelings, facts and the well-being of all involved, *including* yourself.

Lesson Eight Exercises:

1. Rate yourself on a scale of 1 to 10 on how confident you feel (1 being the least confident and 10 being the most confident). Be totally honest.

   Write down the reasons for your selection and identify the top five areas you're most confident in and the top five areas you're least confident in. It's important to see these written out on paper.

   Then list three things you can do to improve your confidence in each of the five weaker areas. These do not need to be business specific. How we feel about ourselves in our everyday lives directly impacts the confidence we have in our business. If you're not confident about your weight, for example, maybe it will hold you back from posting photos of yourself or networking with other women. Address these areas so you can learn to truly love and accept yourself or make the necessary changes in order to make that happen.

2. Are there common areas in the list above where you lack confidence? Are there any others I haven't mentioned? Write down specifically how you'll work on these areas so that you no longer lack confidence in them.

3. Write a letter to yourself from the most confident version of your future self and address all your insecurities that you no longer have. How do you feel as the most confident version of yourself? What will you be able to achieve as this new and improved boss lady?

4. Write a list of everyone you admire who is living the life you dream of.

   Make an honest effort to reach out to them for advice. Don't forget to offer them something in exchange for their time. Remember, you get what you pay for.

The Million Dollar Bakery

Chapter Twelve

Lesson Nine: Start Creating the Life of Your Dreams Today

All the success I've had boils down to one thing. That's right *one*.

Taking. Fucking. *Action*.

There's literally no better way to get shit done than by getting shit done. Waiting does *not* make you money, and it doesn't get you closer to your goals. Shocking, I know. Your business should constantly be in motion moving towards something, whether that means implementing new systems or strategies, developing new marketing plans, expanding, opening a new store—whatever. Fact is, if you allow yourself an extended period of time without taking the next action step, you're entering the ugly old comfort zone with its dirty shag carpet and green crushed velvet drapes from 1962. Don't allow yourself to get to a comfortable spot with your business and just coast along unless that's what your goal is. No businesses grow by *coasting*. It'll stay right where it is or if it does grow, it will not be substantial. If that's what you want, then fine… But, if you want more money, more freedom and to achieve greatness, you'd better get your body into motion girlfriend!

Once you've accomplished something or worked on developing one area of your business, ask yourself, *What's next?* OK, make sure you celebrate the accomplishments with a glass of wine, but *What's next?* should be at the bottom of the glass.

While you're growing your business and developing new strategies, don't take your attention off of the #1 most important part. Do you remember what I told you it was? Sales. Never be so distracted by development that you let your sales slide. If need be, pause whatever you're working on, stabilize the sales and then get back to development.

Don't underestimate the need to adapt and pivot your business to fit the evolving needs of your customers, economy or market. Nothing proved this more than when we pulled Chick Boss Cake through COVID-19 in 2020. If you've done this, you understand the importance of circumstantial evolution. COVID-19 aside, pivoting is essential to the growth and longevity of your business. The market is always changing, and your customers are always evolving. If you don't grow *with* them, they'll outgrow *you*.

Adopt healthy habits and make sure you're taking the utmost care of yourself. It's easy to let the business *run you* but take it from me, the business will only be as healthy as the leader. Investing in yourself *always* pays off—I promise. It's not sustainable to operate by putting yourself second in business or in life—*ever*. It's only a matter of time before the unhealthy eating, lack of routine, disorganization and stress catch up with you. And kills you, my friend. Much earlier than you anticipate. You owe it to your business, your partner, your kids and most importantly to yourself to take the best possible care of yourself. A healthy lifestyle makes you an overall better person for them too.

I know that you *know* what your true calling is and what you're *meant* to do. You can pretend like you don't but that's just a safety mechanism to keep you locked in your comfort zone. Your purpose, your gift and what you *should* be doing with your life is in your heart. You already know what it is. Find the courage to pursue it and share it with the world. The world *needs* what you have to offer, and it needs more passionate, fulfilled people living the life of their dreams and fewer people filling corporate roles with the dull lackluster spark of hope found in looking forward to the weekend.

Never in my wildest dreams did I imagine that Chick Boss Cake could ever reach the level of success it has. I mean, that's the whole reason why I had always believed that I needed to have a *real* job or a real career in some field that society deemed acceptable. I can't help but to reflect on this incredible business I've built from a small side hustle hobby in my tiny apartment kitchen to this locally successful business that's reached over a million in sales. Even more, I can't fathom how a woman who didn't have a clue what she was doing any step of the way, with no formal education, who moved out on her own at sixteen could possibly build such a successful business. I couldn't fathom it, but here I am writing a book on how I did it. Yep, *me* writing a book. No English major and no idea how to "properly" do it. I haven't even thought about how to publish it yet. I just did the same thing I've told you to do throughout: take action and start with the most logical step first—*actually writing the book*. Figure the rest out later. This is just another piece of irony in my legacy of how a high school dropout with nothing but fire in her soul and desire to achieve greatness despite her past can build a million-dollar bakery business and write a freaking book about it!

I know in my heart and soul that if I can move mountains to create the life of my dreams, you can too! Thinking back on that very first conversation in the Tim Hortons parking lot in my old Mustang, I cannot imagine what my life would be like today had I fallen victim to my fears and chosen the *safer* route. One thing I know for certain is that I'd be living a *very* different life filled with broken dreams and untapped potential. There'd be a Chick but sadly, no Boss and no Cake. That chick would be unfulfilled, searching for happiness and struggling trying to find herself. Finding yourself is never guaranteed, and you could be left searching *forever*. Creating yourself, on the other hand, is a sure-fire way to go after your goals and turn your dreams into a reality!

Where will you be in a few years time if you decide to take action and start *today*?

Would it change your life?

What's the worst that could happen?

Let me tell you what's the worst that could happen: you end up back where you currently *are* today. How does being back to where you're at today scare you from chasing your dreams? You'll always have the option to come back to this place if you choose to, but you'll never know what you could have become if you don't take the opportunity right now to see what you could be missing out on. If you don't chase your dreams now, you'll still be where you are today regardless, so why not just try?

Your new life is only going to cost you your old one, so if you're prepared to make that trade for bigger and better things then stop *waiting*. Start *doing*. Now!

Turn your ordinary life into something extraordinary and start creating the life of your dreams today!

Lesson Nine Exercises:

1. Create the life of your dreams. Literally. Right now, write down your ideal life and be extremely audacious! Don't hold anything back and be extremely specific in what a day in the life and a year in the life looks like for your best future self. Is it travelling the world, working from your beautiful Pinterest-worthy home office with views of NYC out your window? What are you wearing, what do you look like, who do you hang out with, what kind of friends do you have? Describe it all. If you're an artsy person you could even create a vision board of what it looks like and display it in plain sight.

   I cannot stress the importance of this enough: you need to identify what you want and what your dreams look like. Get creating and then start doing!

2. Action Jackson. What do you need to do in order to achieve the life you've created above? More free time? More money? Both? If that's the case, then laser focus on how you can get more time and more money. Let this be the motivator for you when you don't think you can push any further. Remember why you started, where you're going and that the actions you take will determine the results you get.

   Hint: no action always gets no results.

   You got this, I'm cheering for you!

The Million Dollar Bakery

About The Author

Rebecca Hamilton has created a very successful local bakery business called Chick Boss Cake. It is the #1 bakery and dessert spot that all the locals in southwestern Ontario are obsessed with, and it has a massive following of loyal fans. She's since branched out and created her own personal brand called Rebecca Hamilton Co. (www.rebeccahamiltonco.com) to share her unfiltered, self-taught business knowledge with women around the world in the hopes to impact, inspire and empower them to create the life of their dreams. She runs both businesses anchored by her core values of authenticity, integrity, generosity and kindness. Rebecca hosts her own blog and podcast called *Scrap the Sweet Talk*, where she focuses on sharing her best business and life tips centred around creating the life of your dreams. She's passionate about writing, photography, nature and spending time with her dogs and husband.

Connect with Rebecca

Tune into her podcast called: *Scrap the Sweet Talk*
Follow her on Instagram: @rebeccaatchickbosscake
Follow her bakery on Instagram: @chickbosscake
Take her online courses, read her blog & check out her services at: www.rebeccahamiltonco.com
Visit her bakery at: www.chickbosscake.com